FOR ORGANS, PIANOS & ELECTRONIC KEYBOARDS

E-Z PLAY TODAY

168

CLASSICAL WEDDING FAVORITES

WITHDRAWN

CONTENTS

ISBN 0-634-02598-8

HAL•LEONARD®
CORPORATION
7777 W. BLUEMOUND RD. P.O. BOX 13819 MILWAUKEE, WI 53213

Visit Hal Leonard Online at
www.halleonard.com

Air on the G String
from ORCHESTRAL SUITE NO. 3

Registration 3

By Johann Sebastian Bach

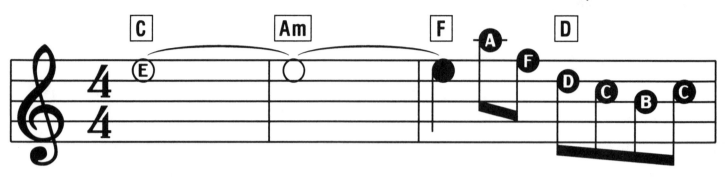

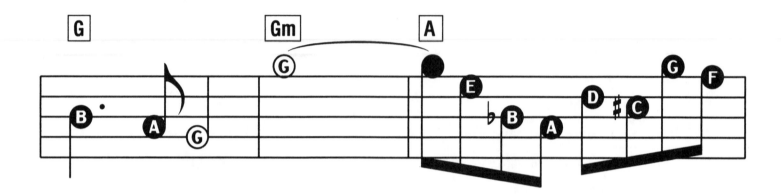

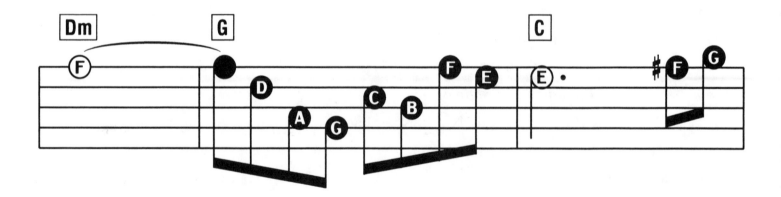

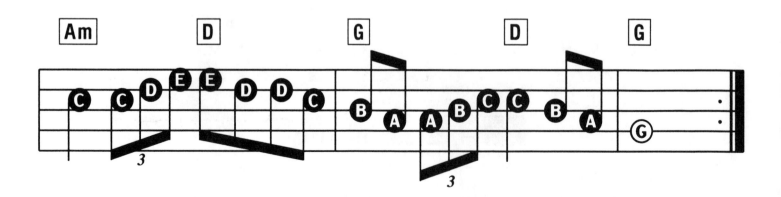

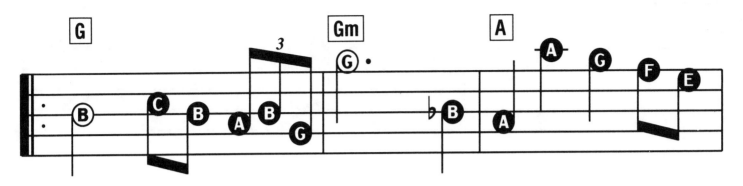

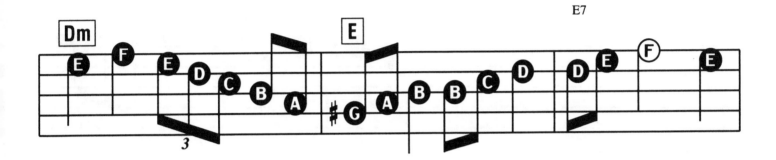

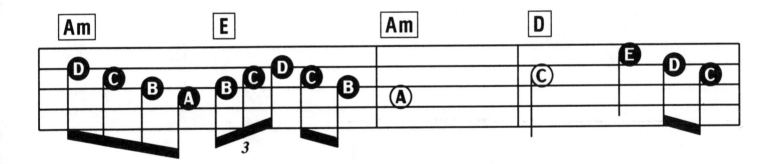

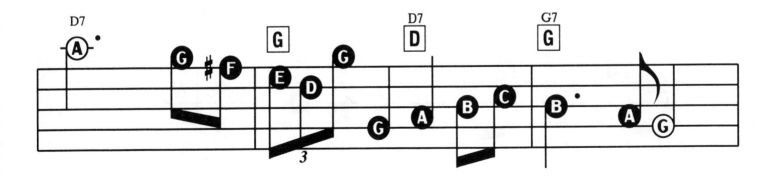

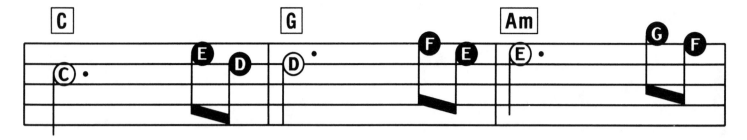

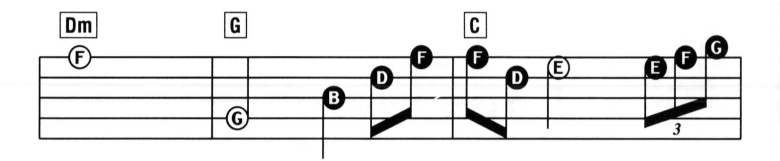

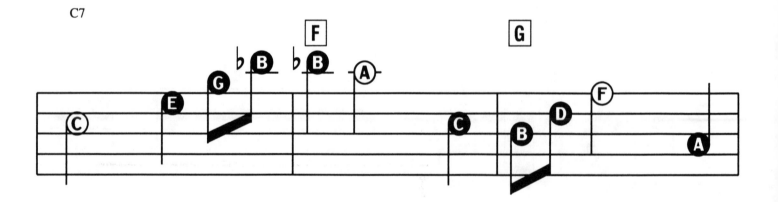

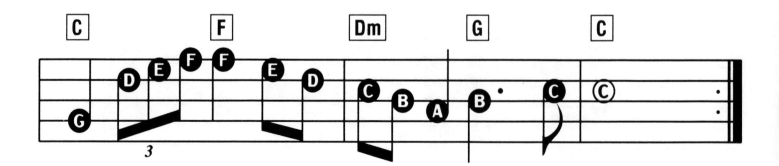

Ave Maria
based on Prelude in C Major by J.S. Bach

Registration 6

By Charles Gounod

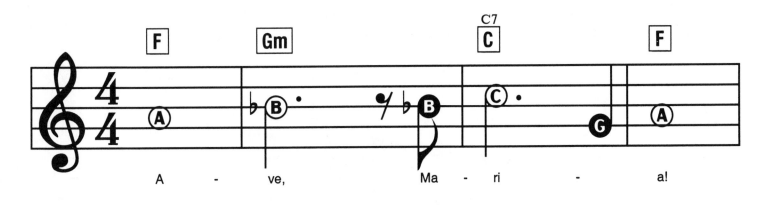

A - ve, Ma - ri - a!

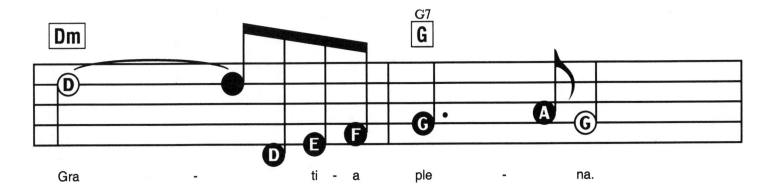

Gra - ti - a ple - na.

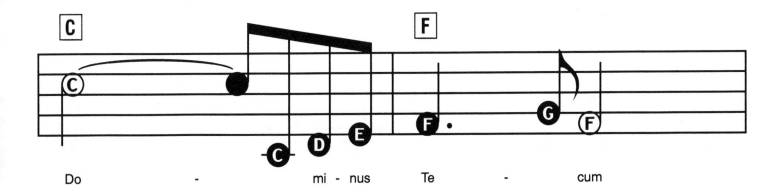

Do - mi - nus Te - cum

be - ne - dic - ta tu in

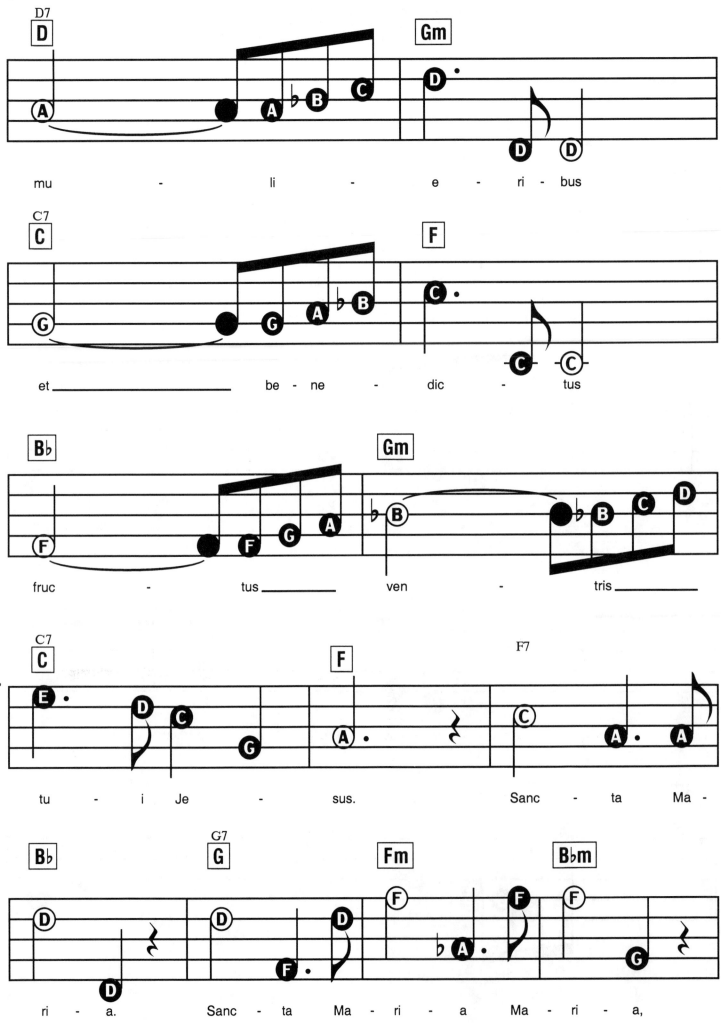

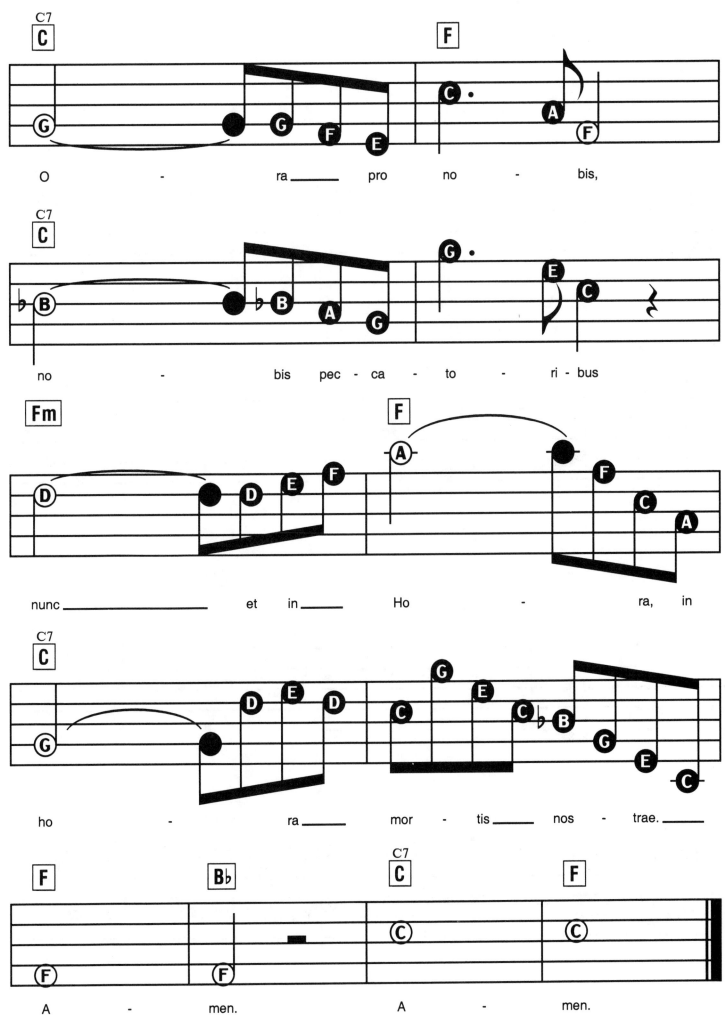

Allegro maestoso
from WATER MUSIC

Registration 4

By George Frideric Handel

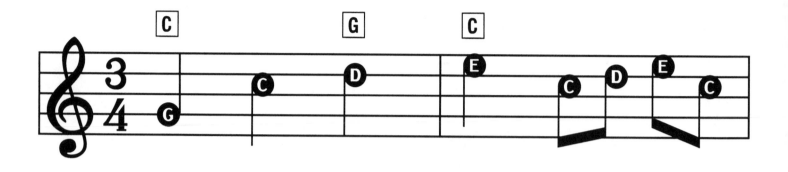

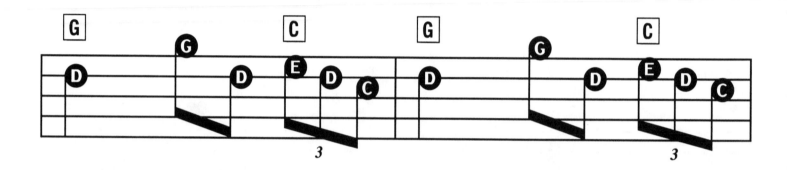

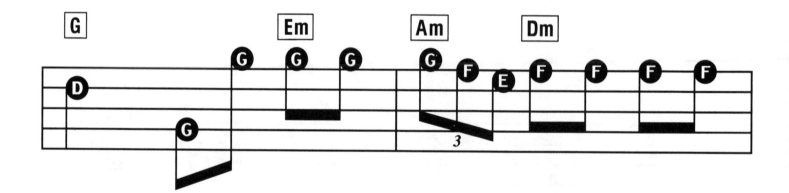

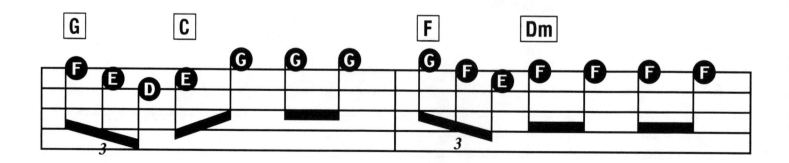

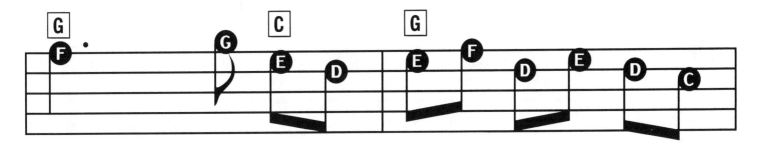

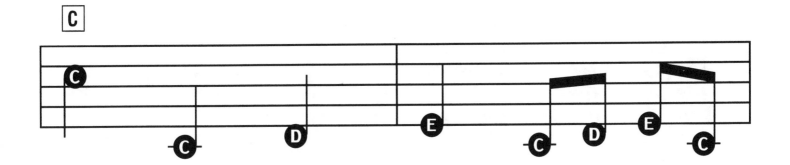

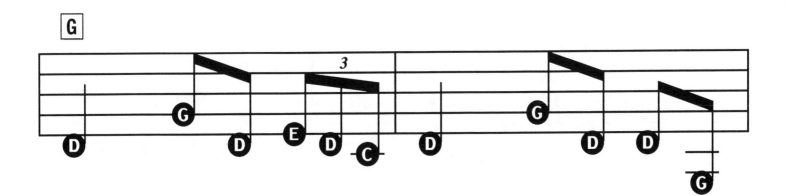

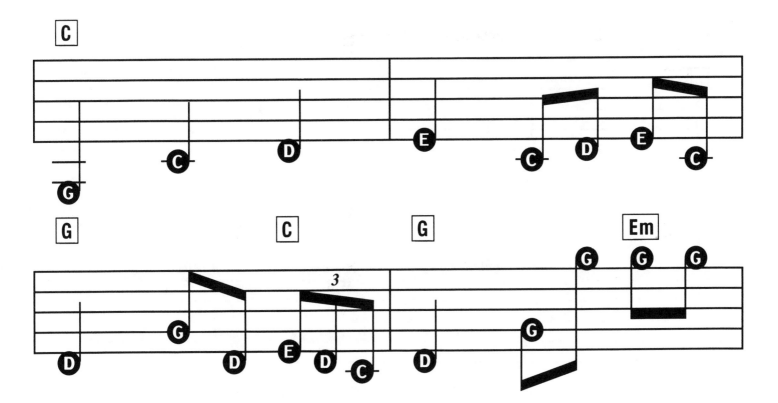

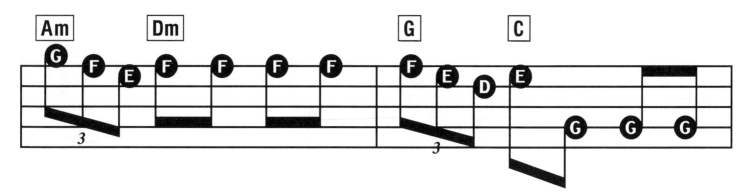

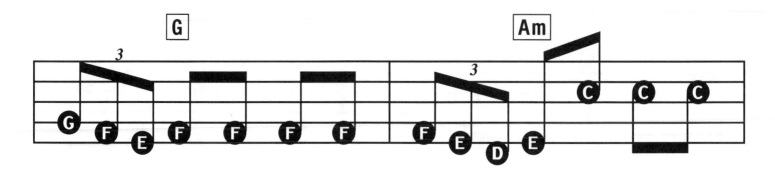

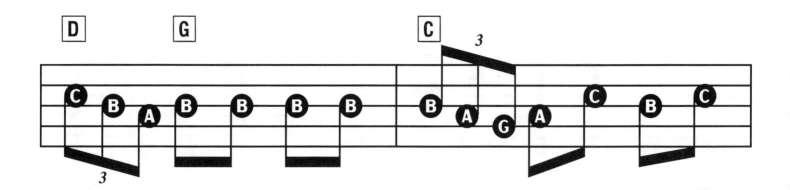

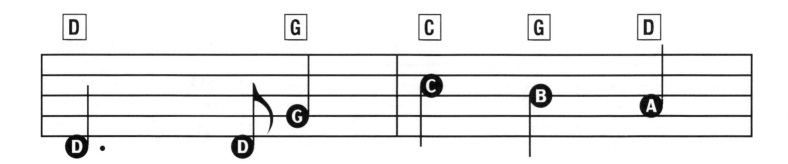

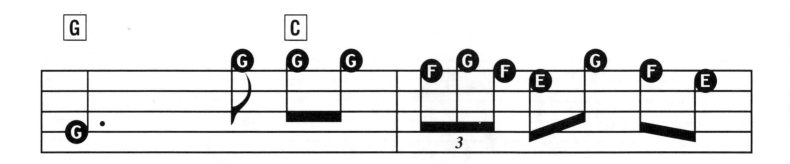

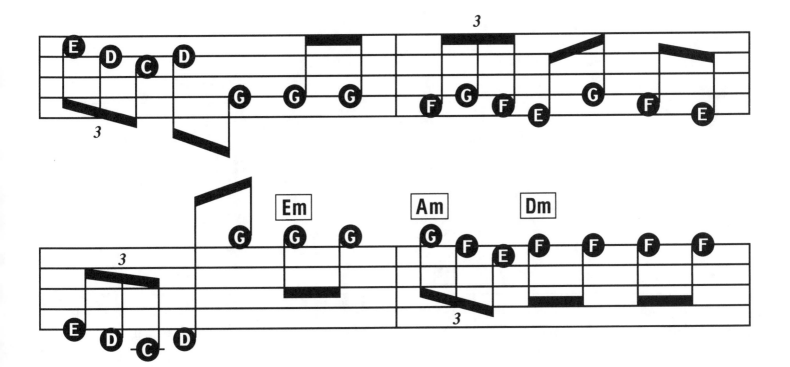

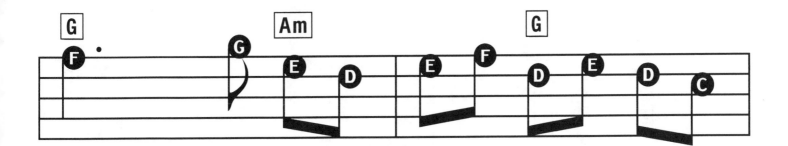

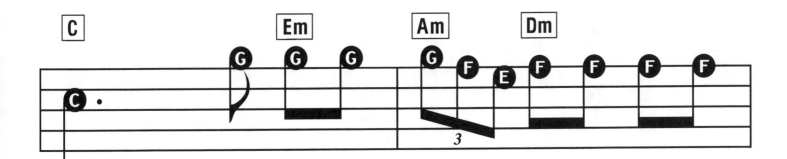

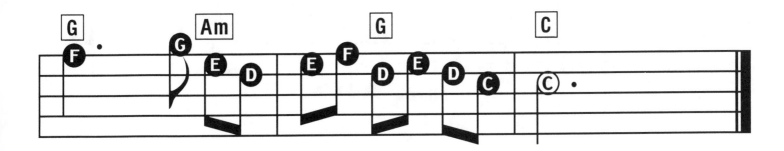

Ave Maria

Registration 6

By Franz Schubert

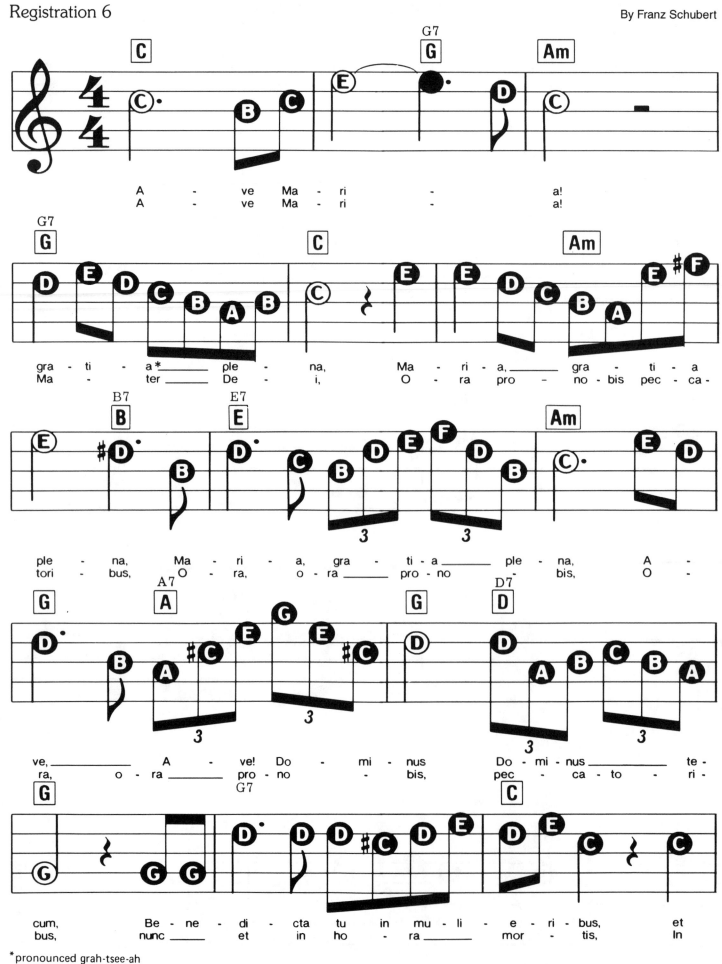

*pronounced grah-tsee-ah

13

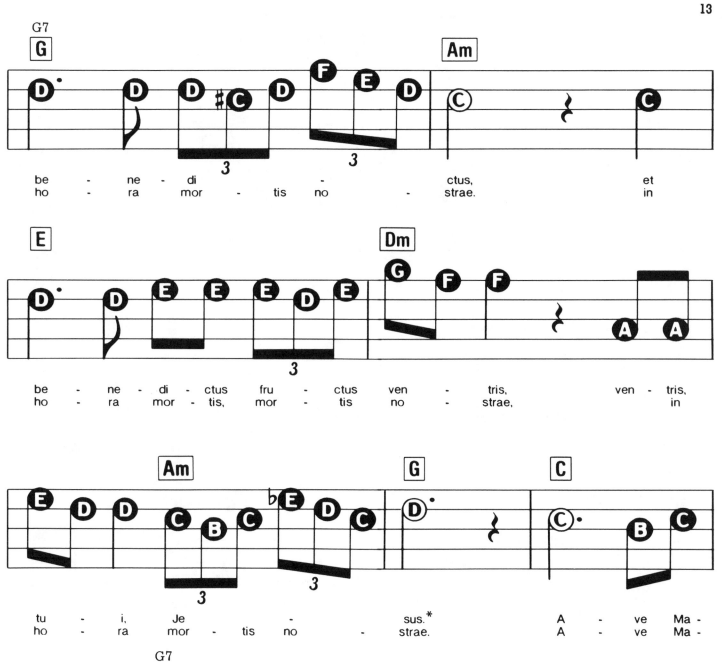

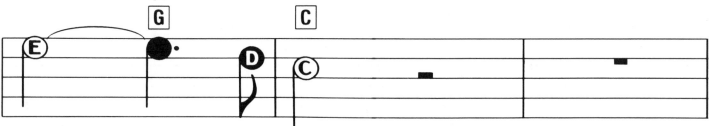

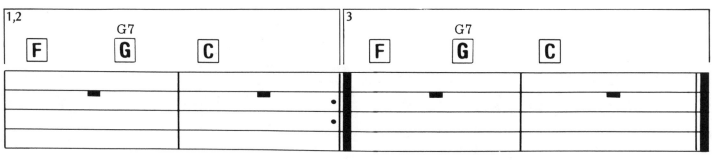

*Pronounced yeh-zoos

Be Thou with Me
(Bist du bei mir)

Registration 3

By Johann Sebastian Bach

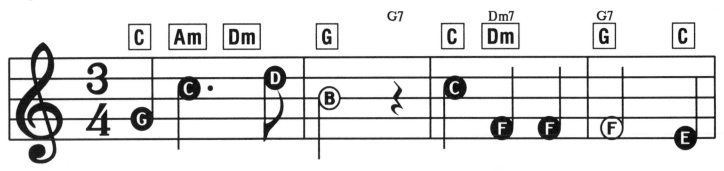

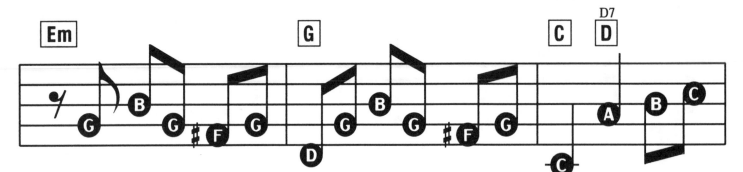

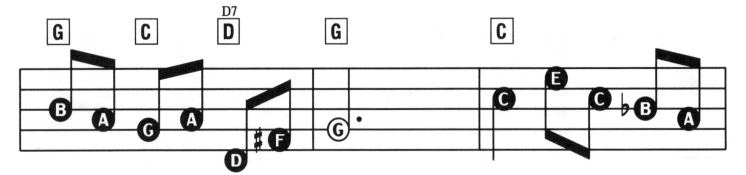

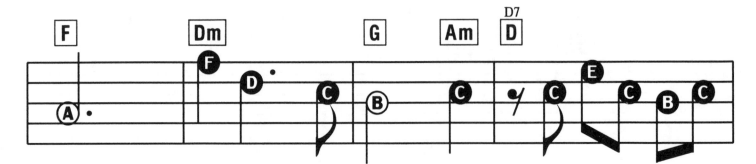

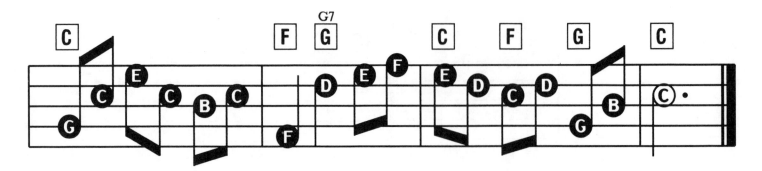

Bridal Chorus
from LOHENGRIN

Registration 2

By Richard Wagner

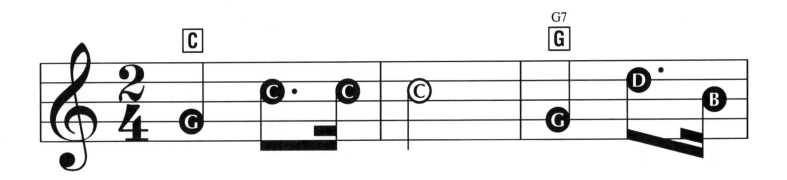

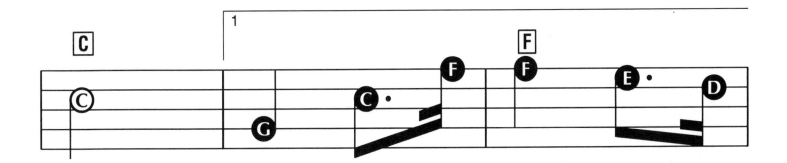

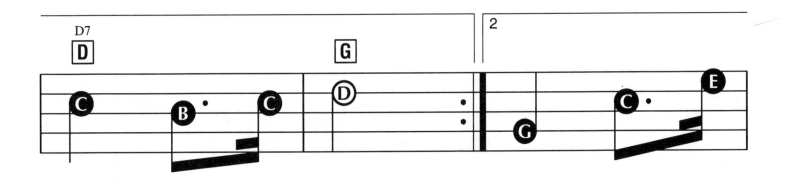

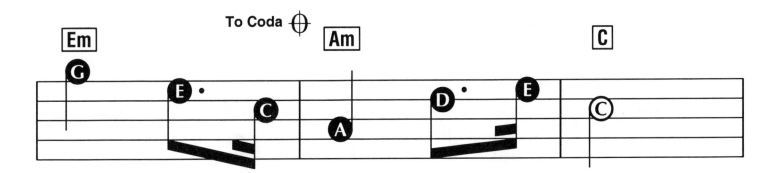

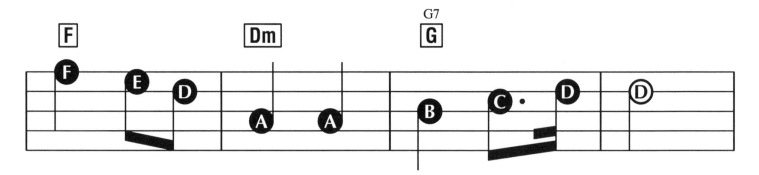

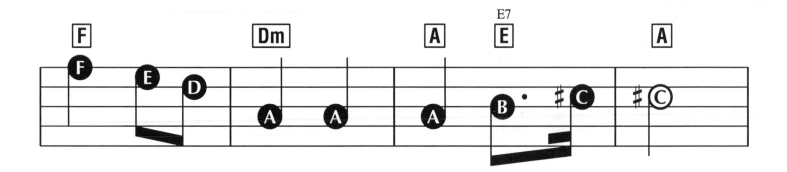

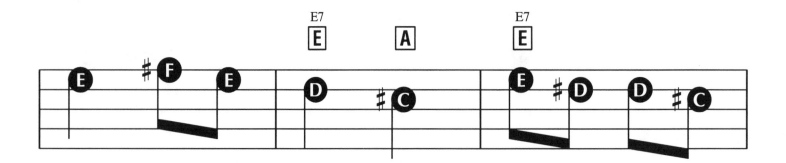

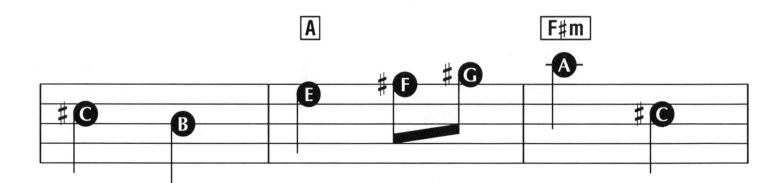

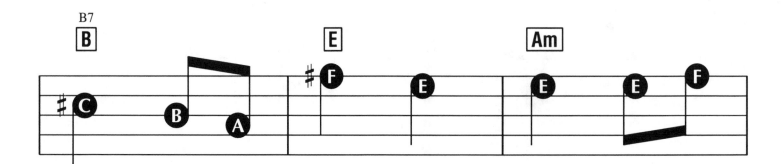

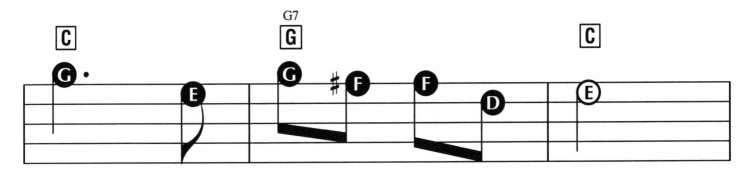

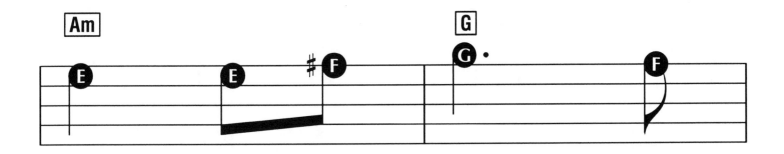

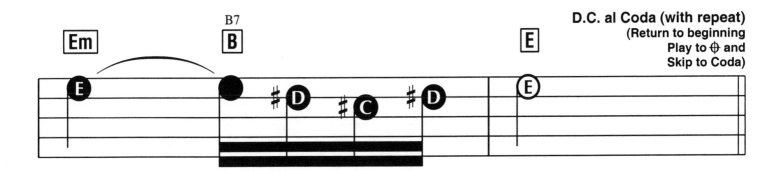

D.C. al Coda (with repeat)
(Return to beginning
Play to ⊕ and
Skip to Coda)

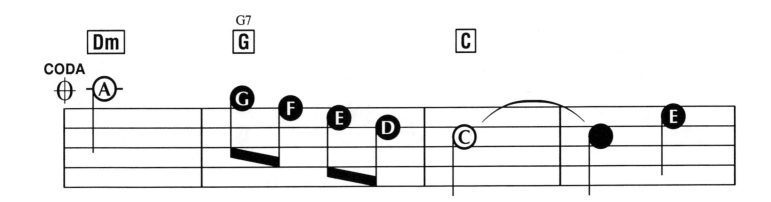

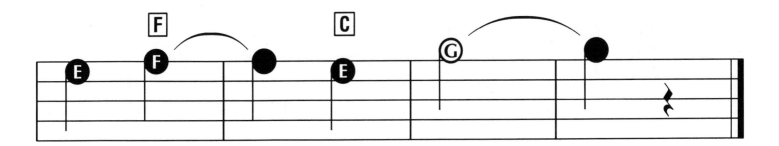

Canon in D Major

Registration 6

By Johann Pachelbel

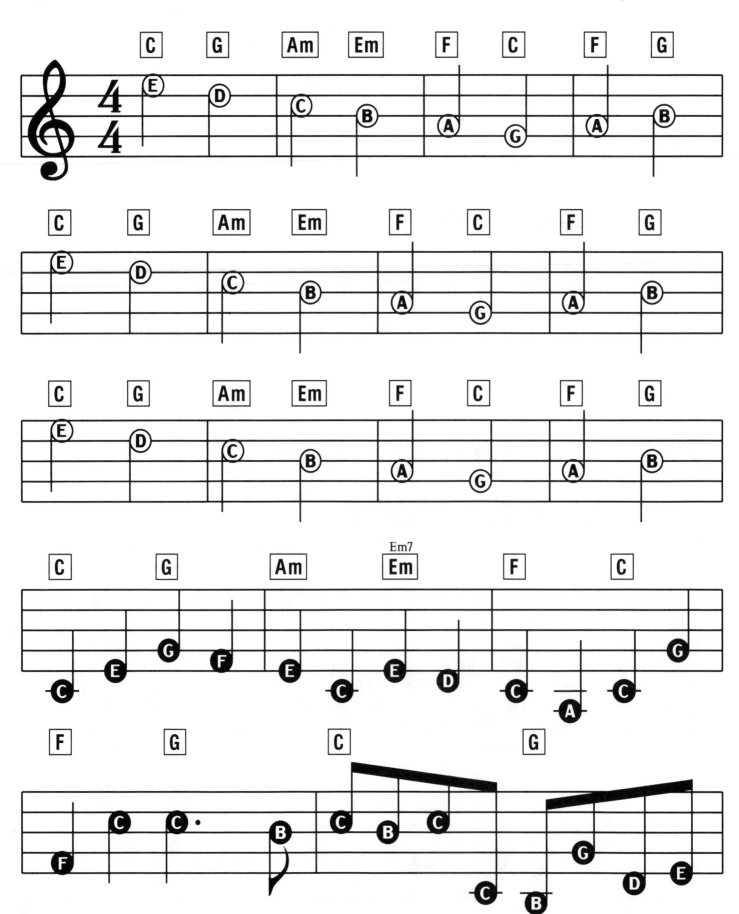

19

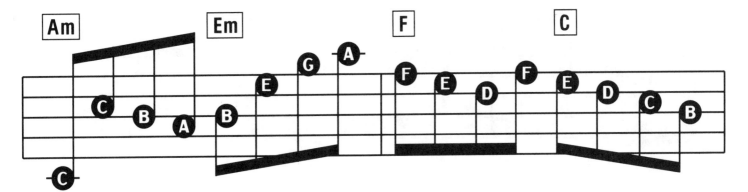

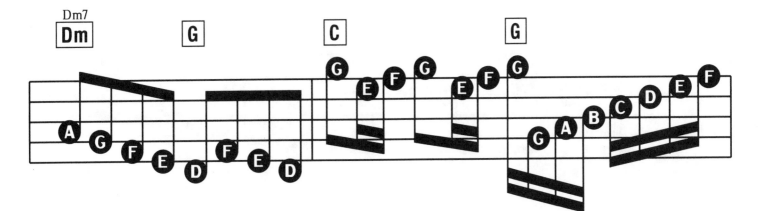

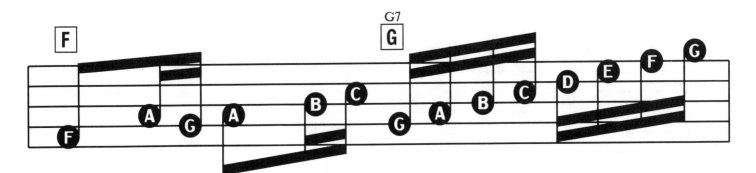

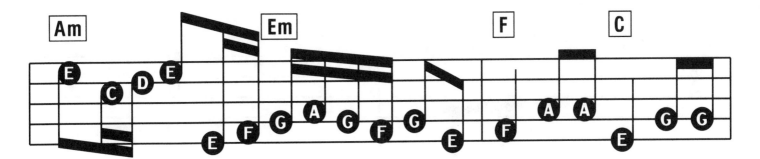

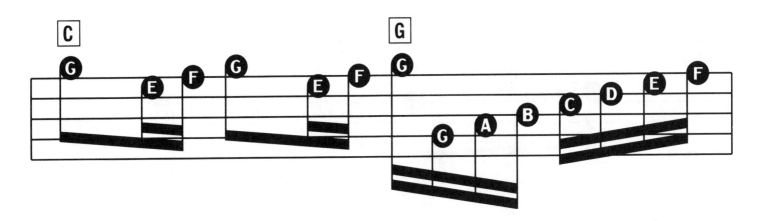

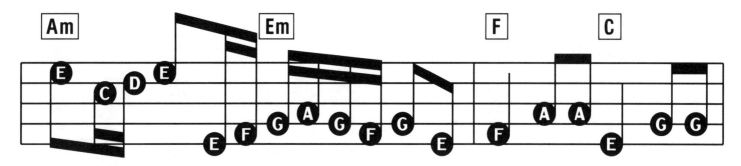

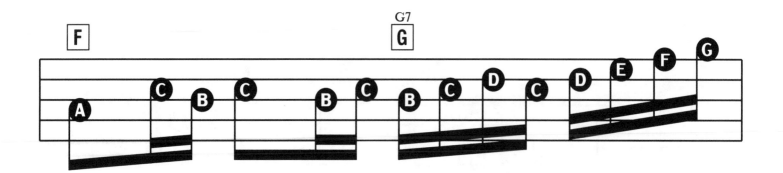

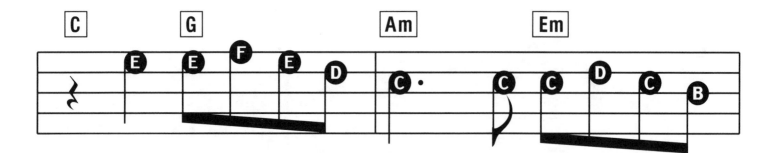

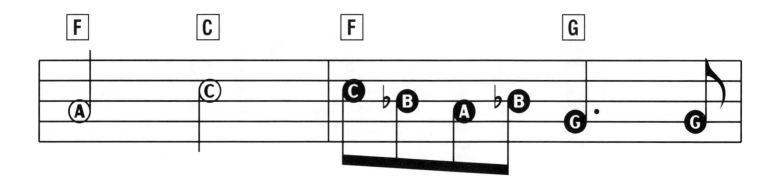

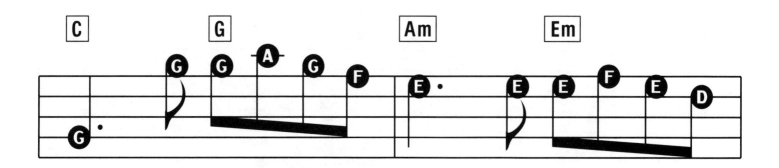

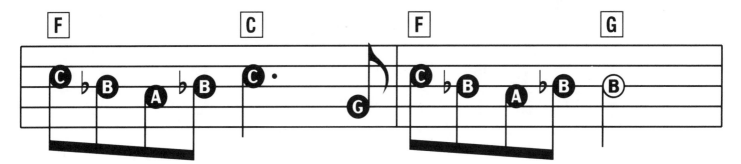

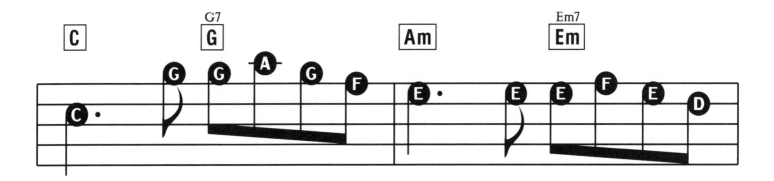

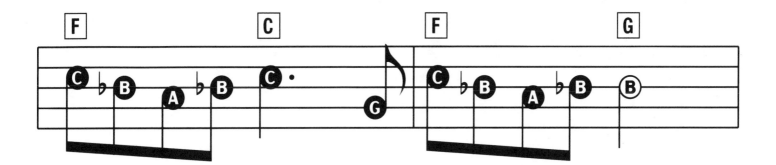

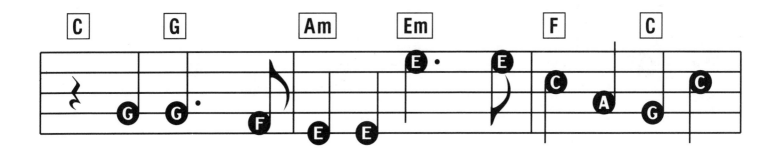

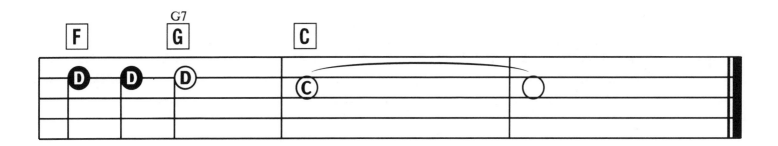

Entreat Me Not to Leave Thee
(Song of Ruth)

Registration 3

Words and Music by
Charles Gounod

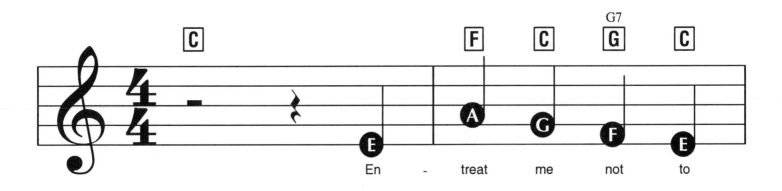

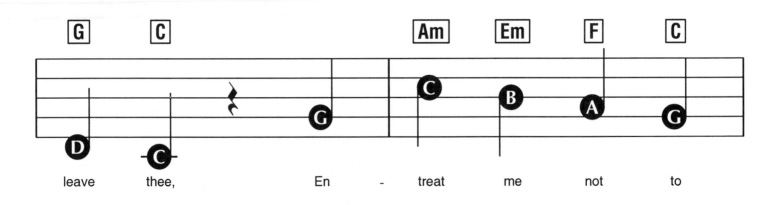

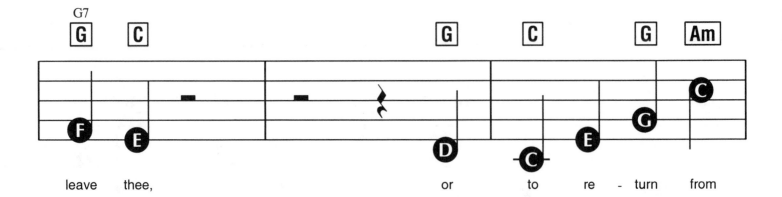

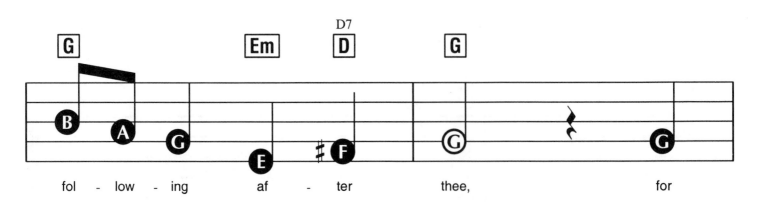

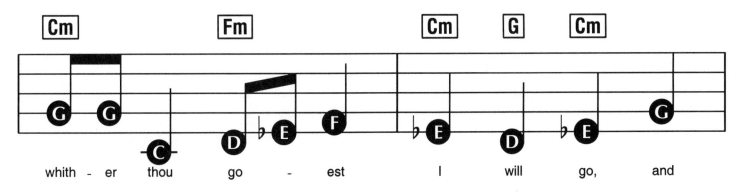

whith - er thou go - est I will go, and

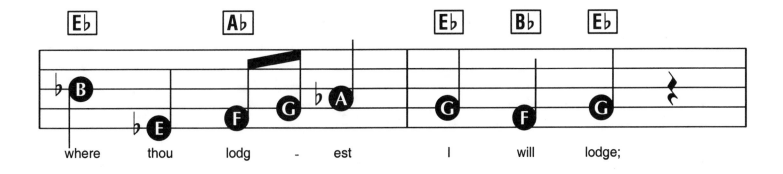

where thou lodg - est I will lodge;

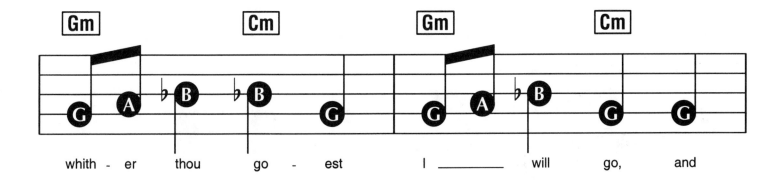

whith - er thou go - est I _____ will go, and

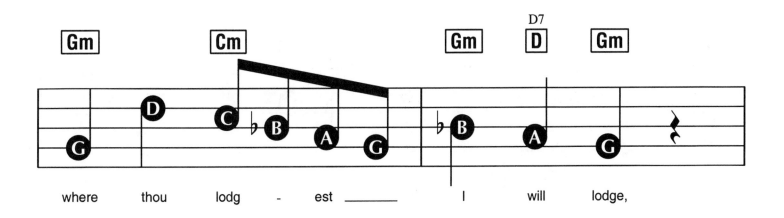

where thou lodg - est _____ I will lodge,

24

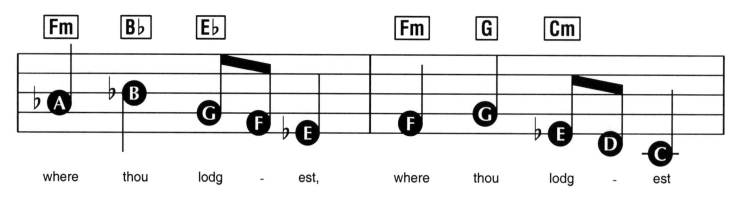

where thou lodg - est, where thou lodg - est

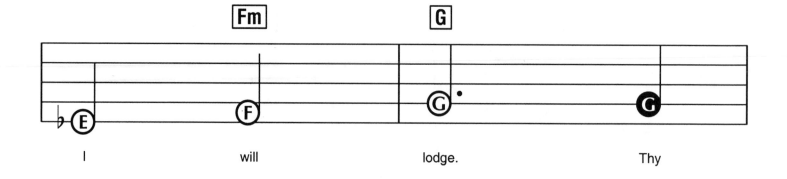

I will lodge. Thy

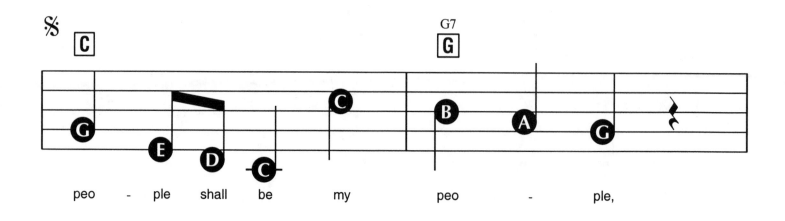

peo - ple shall be my peo - ple,

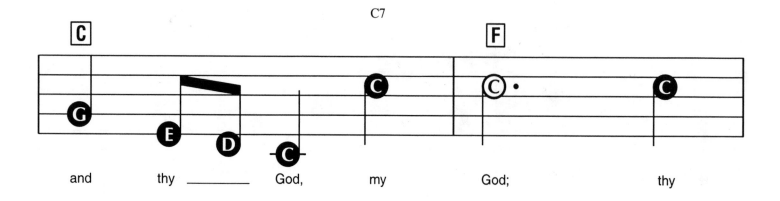

and thy _____ God, my God; thy

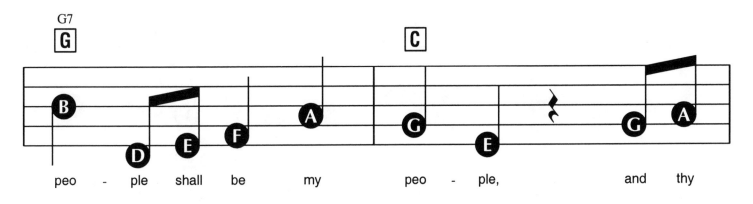

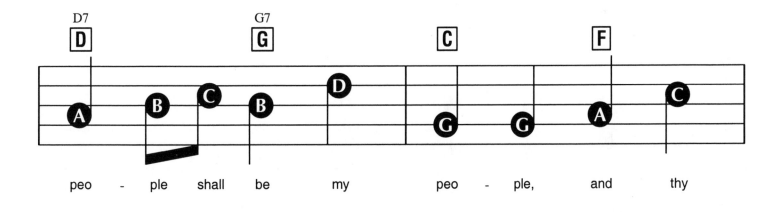

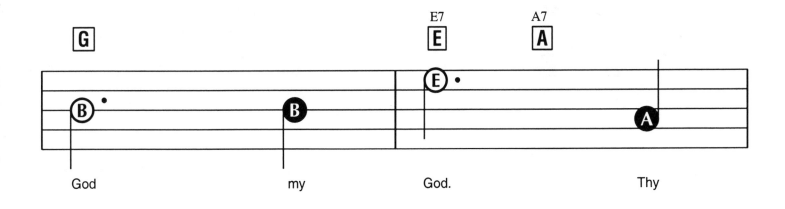

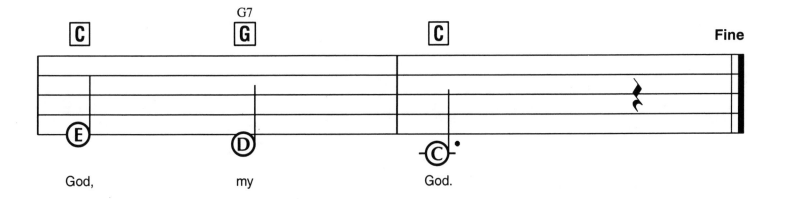

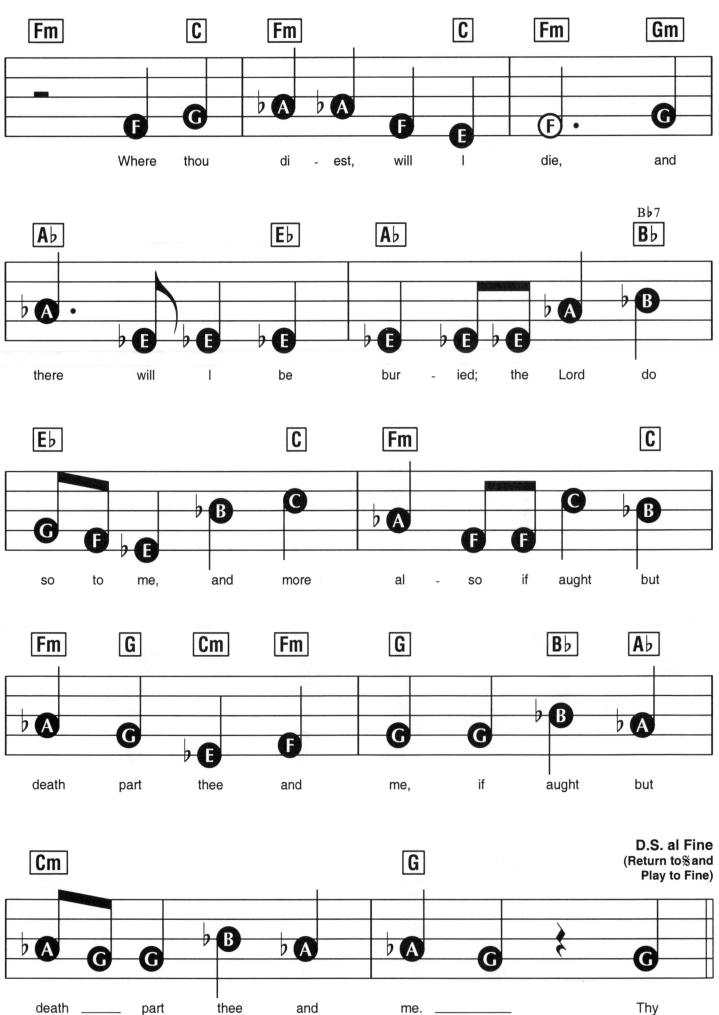

D.S. al Fine
(Return to % and
Play to Fine)

Hornpipe
from WATER MUSIC

Registration 3

By George Frideric Handel

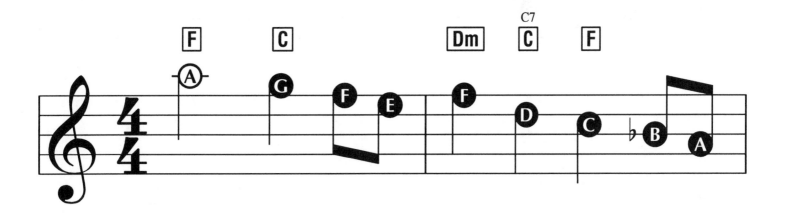

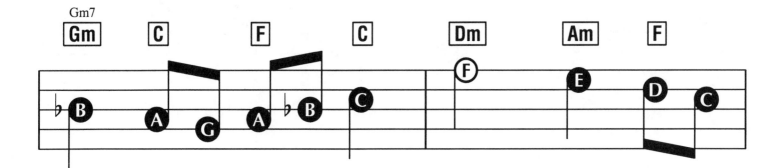

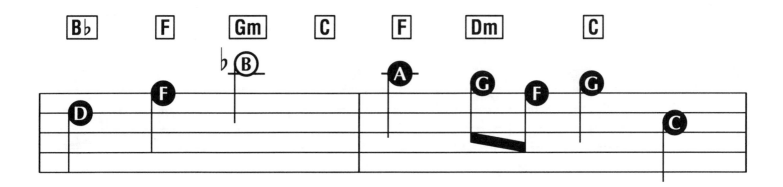

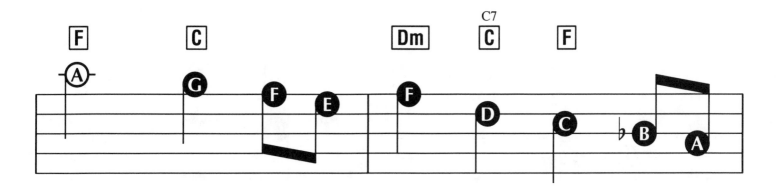

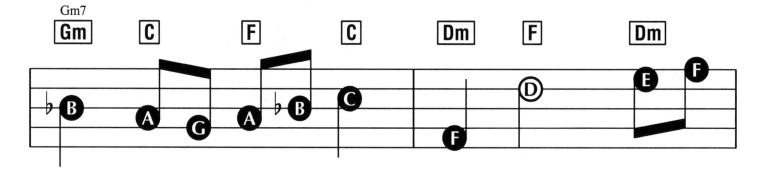

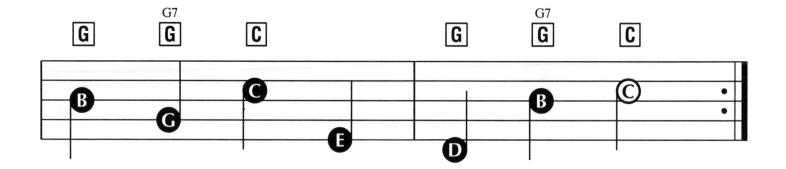

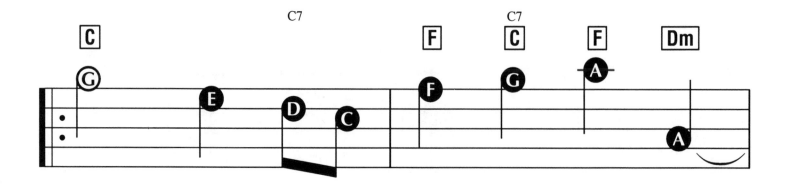

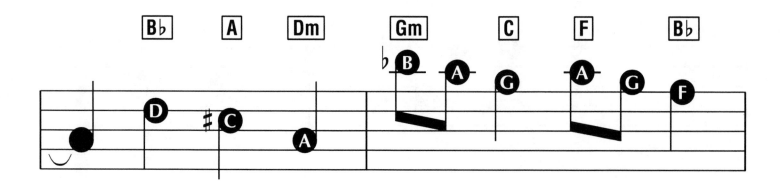

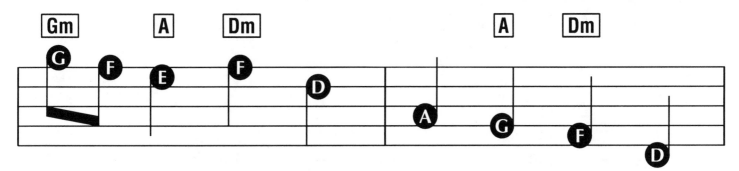

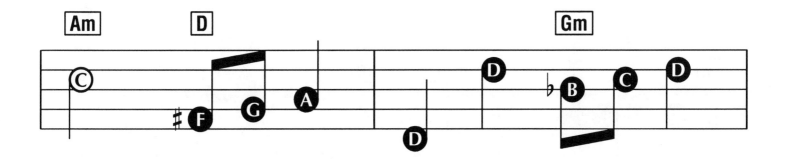

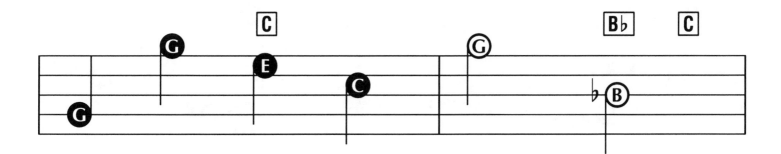

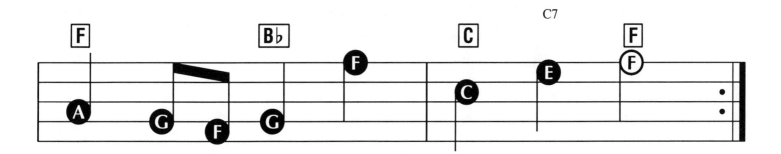

Jesu, Joy of Man's Desiring

Registration 2

By Johann Sebastian Bach

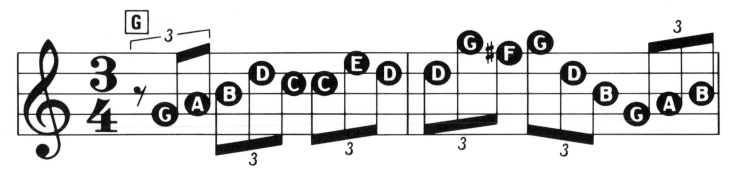

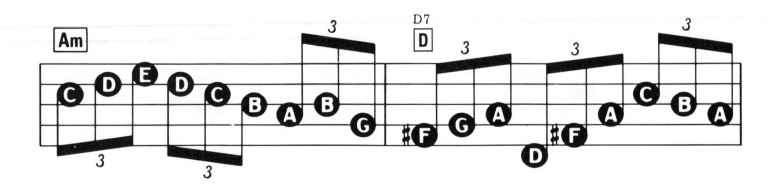

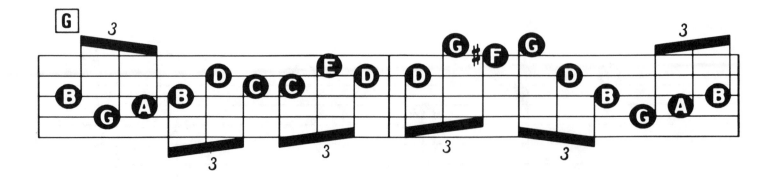

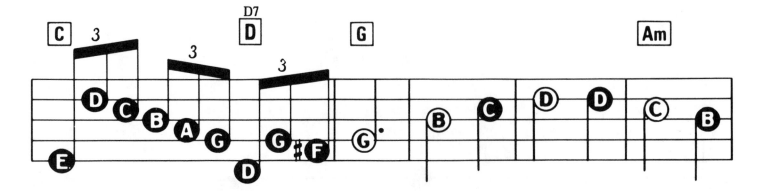

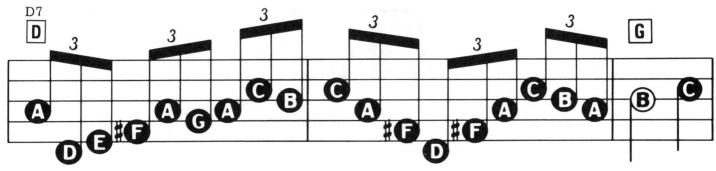

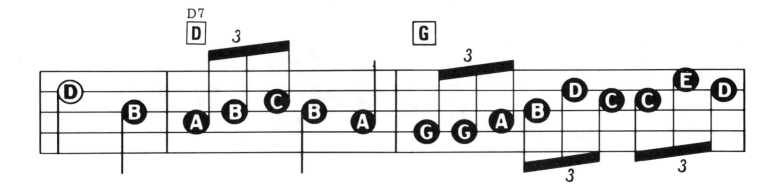

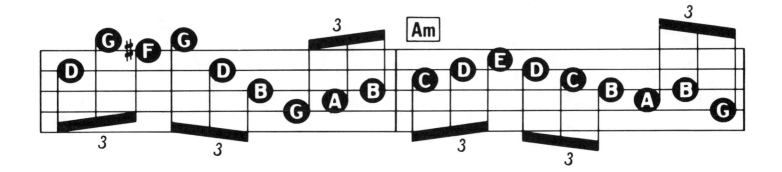

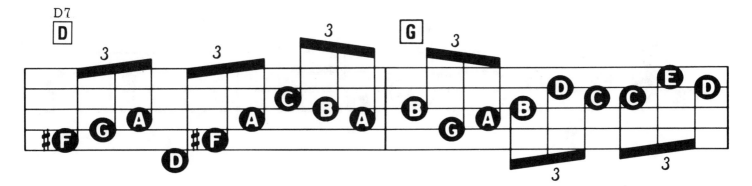

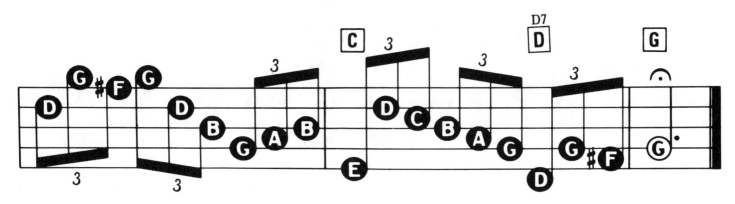

Jupiter
from THE PLANETS
Chorale Theme

Registration 8

By Gustav Holst

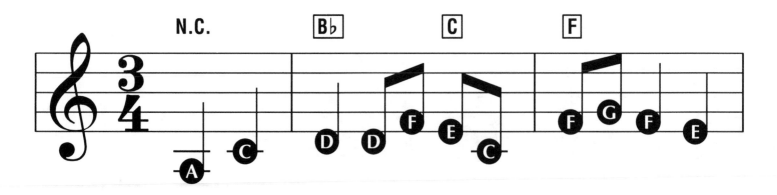

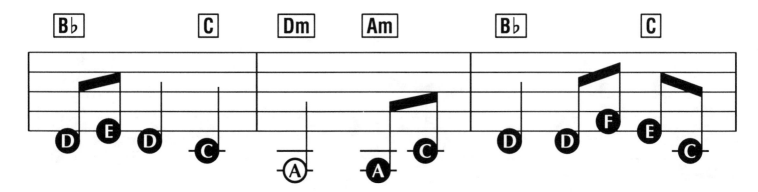

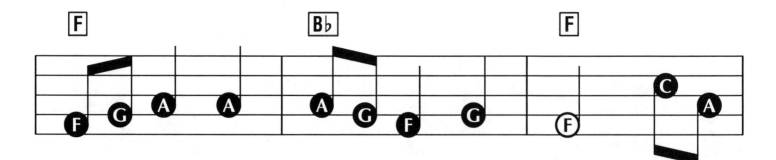

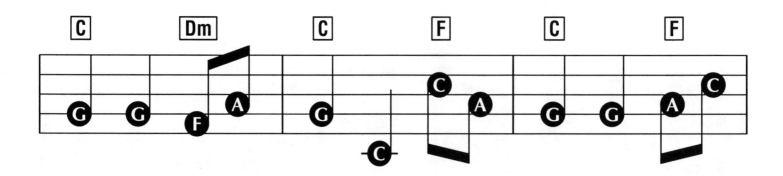

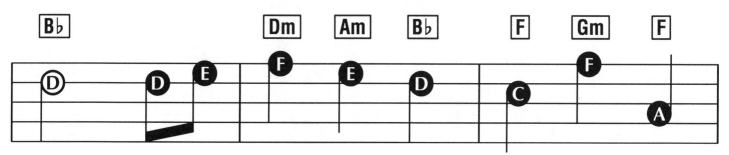

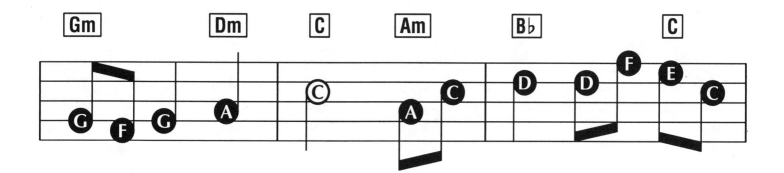

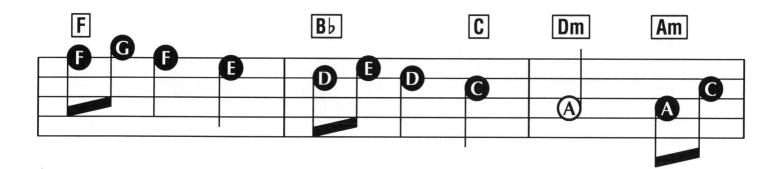

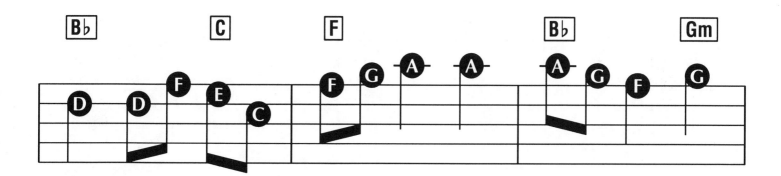

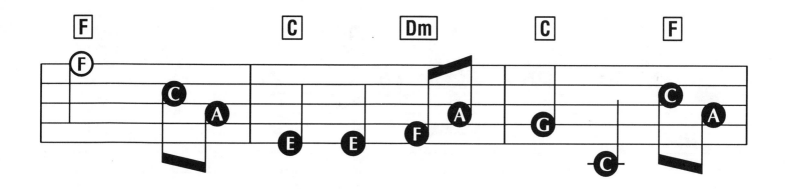

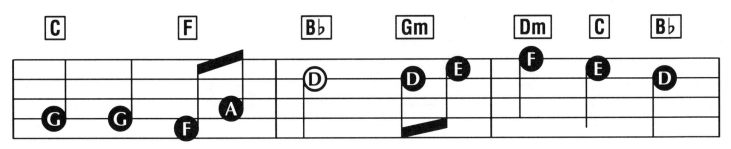

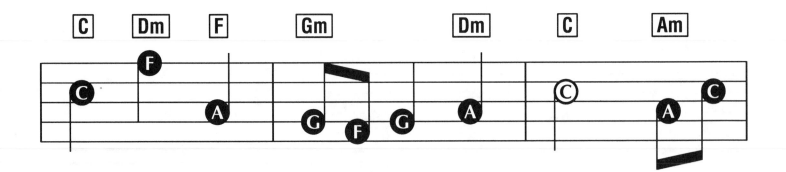

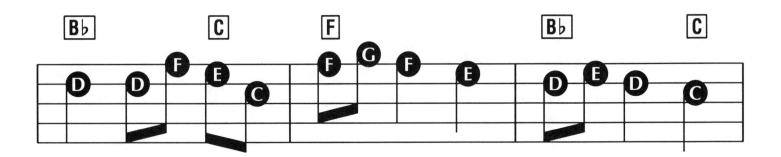

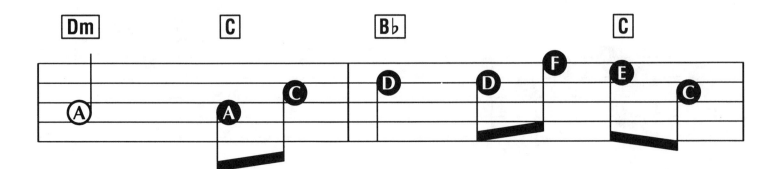

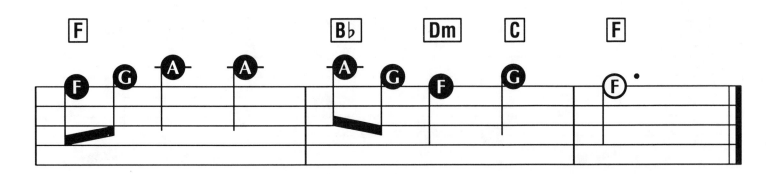

Ode to Joy

from SYMPHONY NO. 9 in D Minor
Fourth Movement Choral Theme

Words by Henry van Dyke
Music by Ludwig van Beethoven

Registration 5

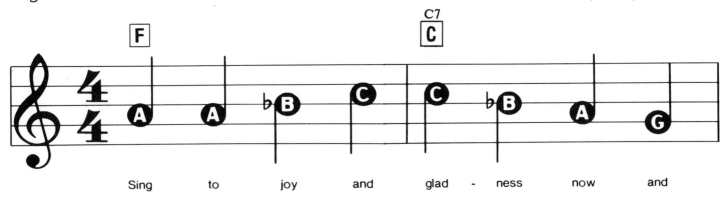

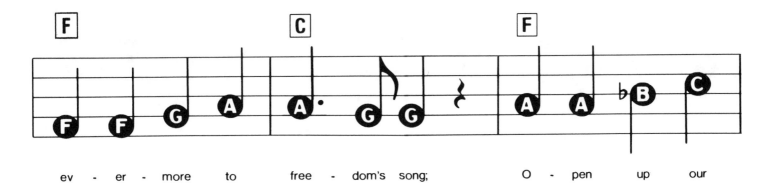

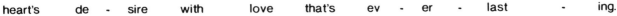

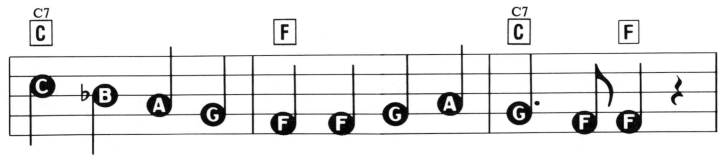

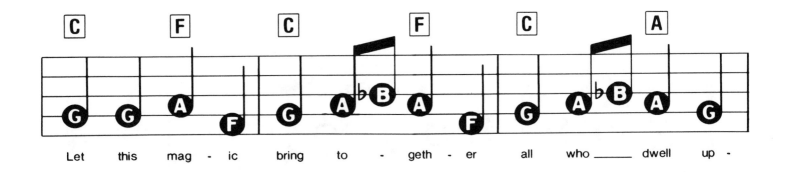

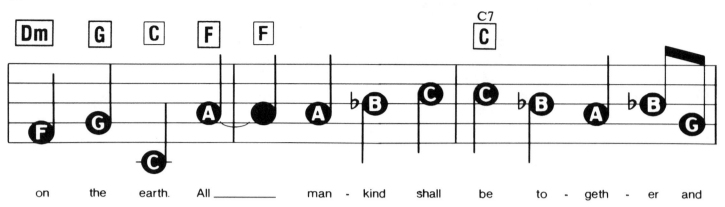

on the earth. All _____ man - kind shall be to - geth - er and

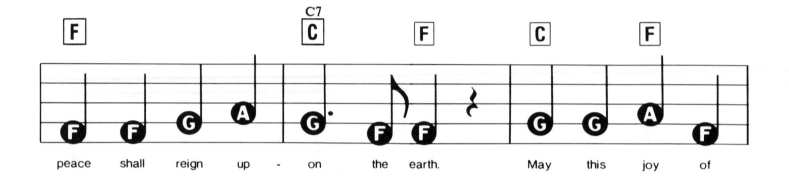

peace shall reign up - on the earth. May this joy of

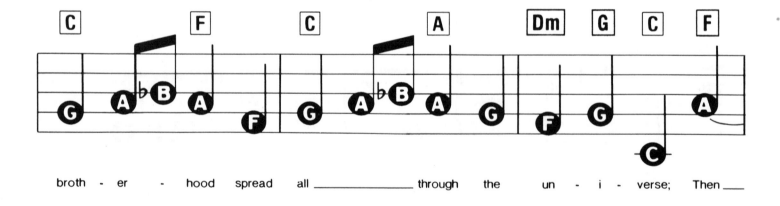

broth - er - hood spread all _____ through the un - i - verse; Then ___

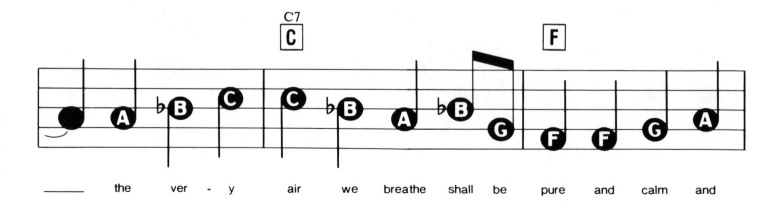

_____ the ver - y air we breathe shall be pure and calm and

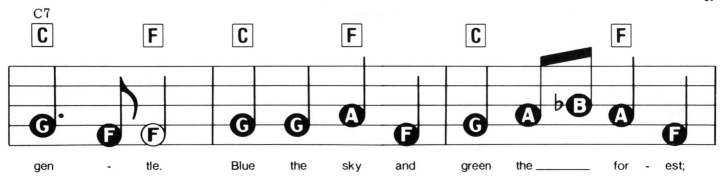

gen - tle. Blue the sky and green the _____ for - est;

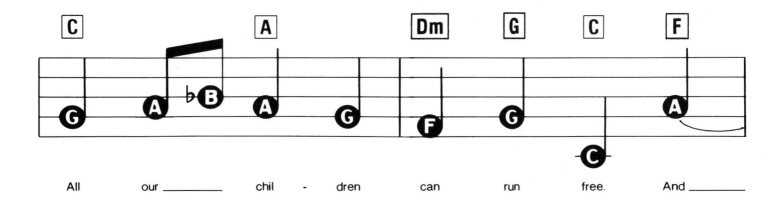

All our _____ chil - dren can run free. And _____

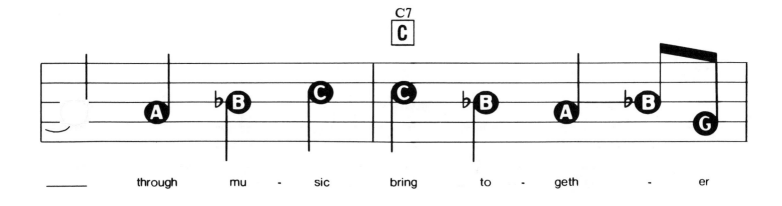

_____ through mu - sic bring to - geth - er

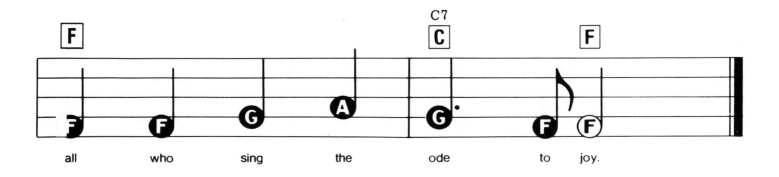

all who sing the ode to joy.

Largo
from XERXES

Registration 3
Rhythm: Waltz

By George Frideric Handel

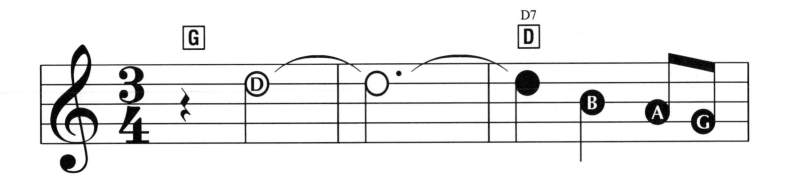

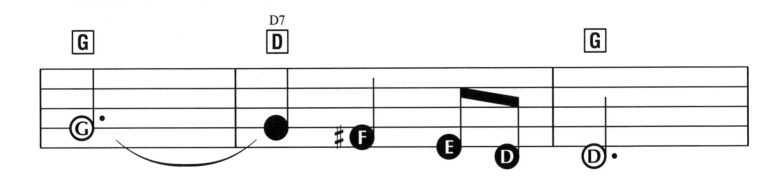

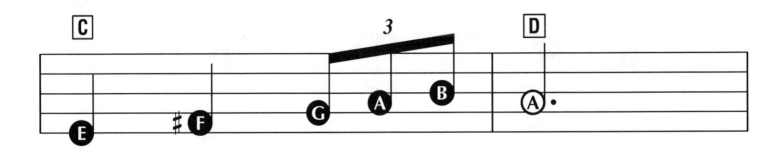

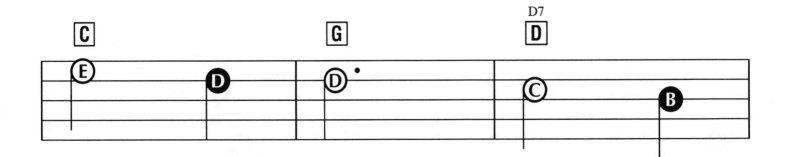

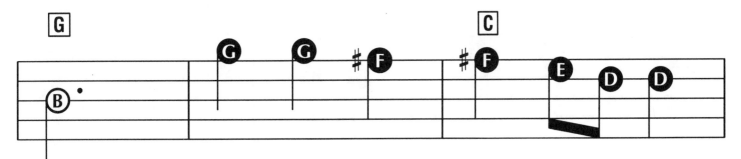

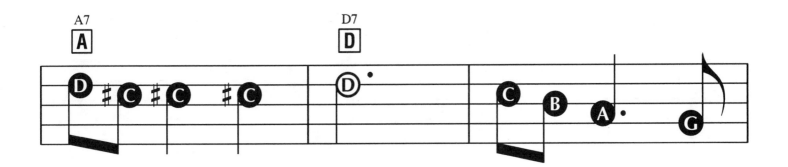

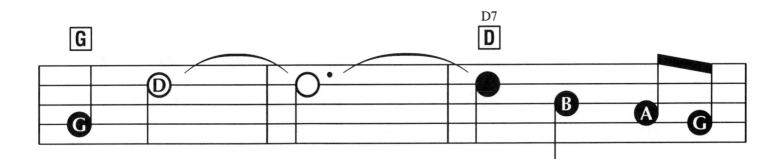

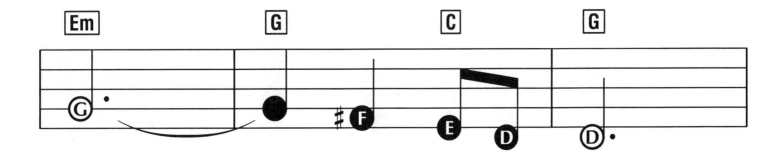

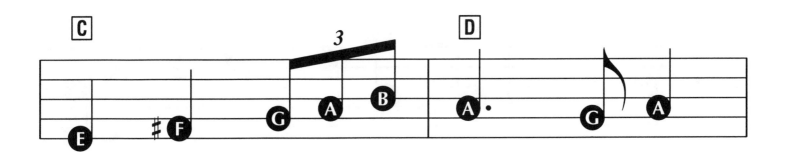

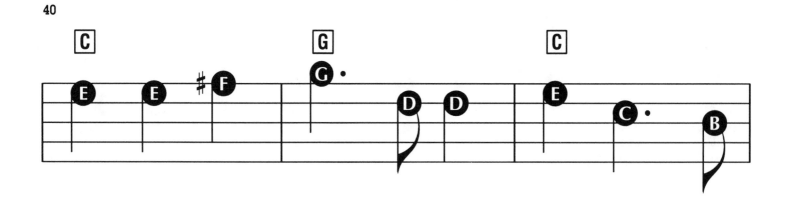

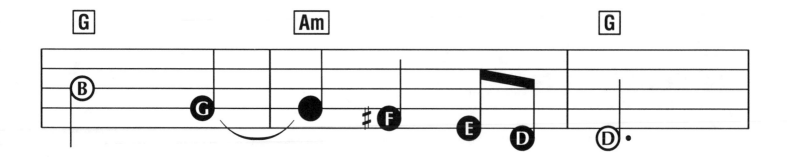

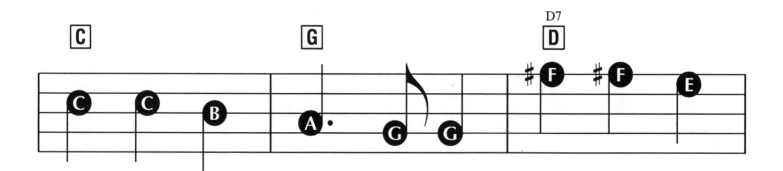

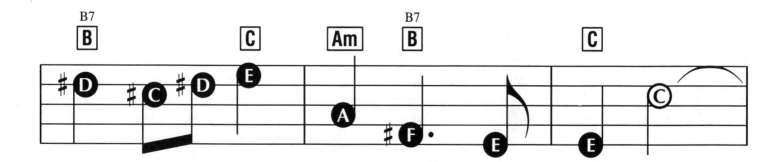

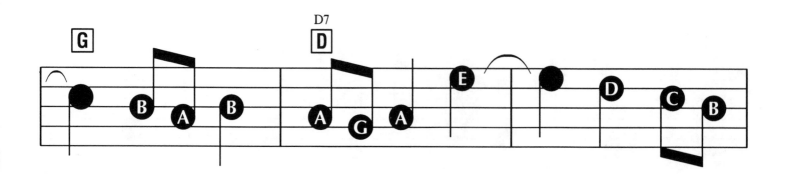

41

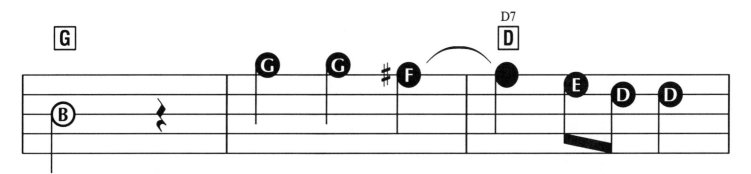

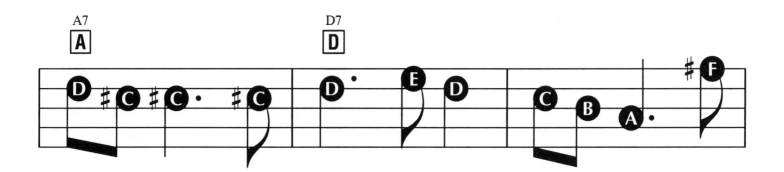

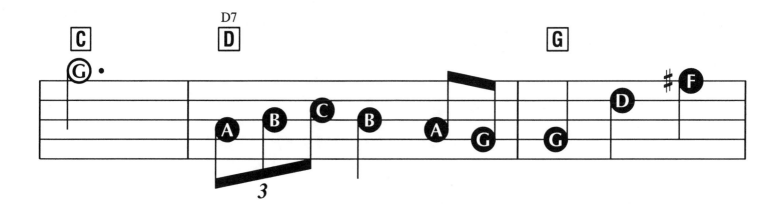

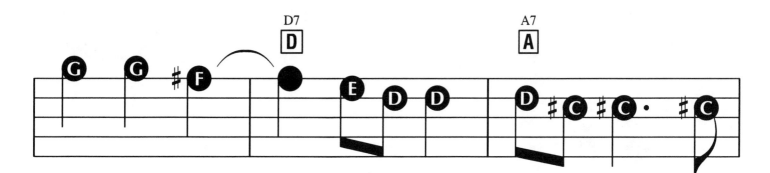

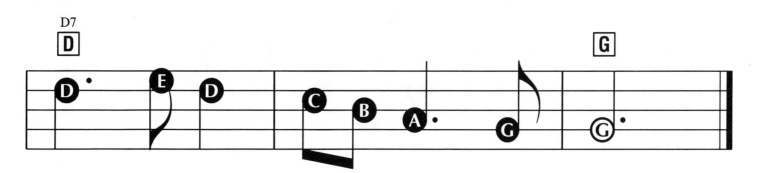

Meditation
from THAÏS

Registration 3

By Jules Massenet

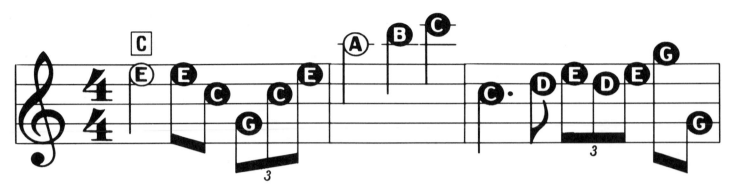

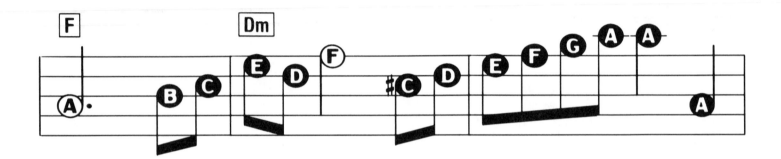

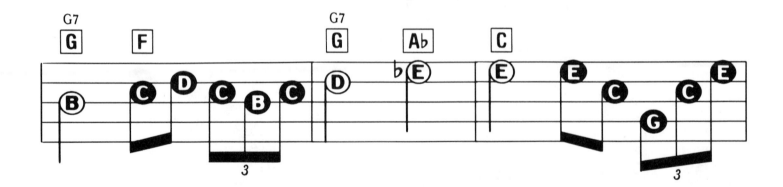

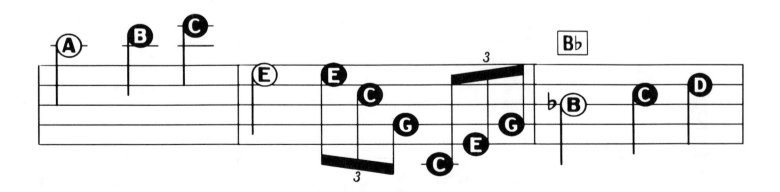

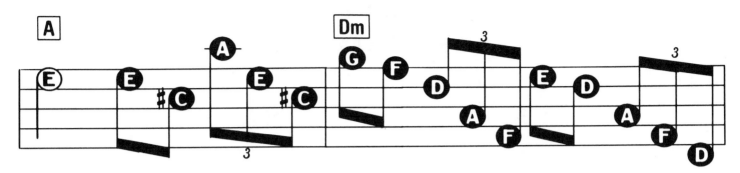
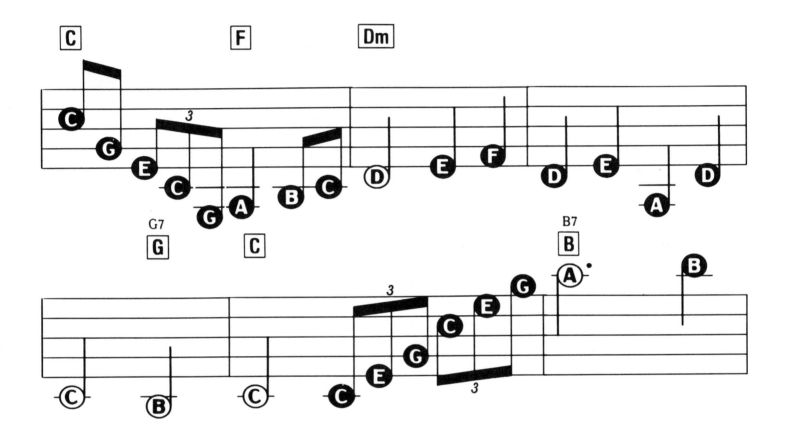
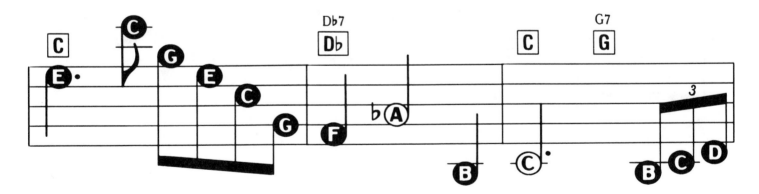
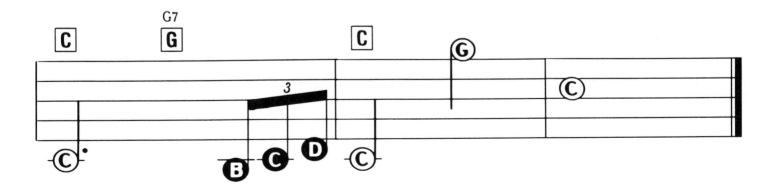

43

My Heart Ever Faithful
from CANTATA 68

Registration 3

By Johann Sebastian Bach

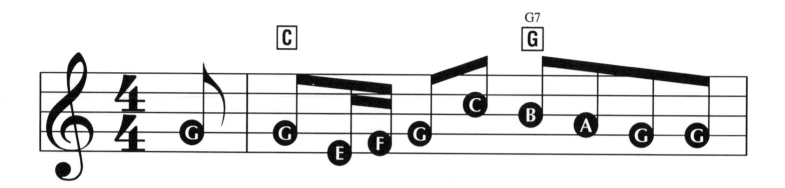

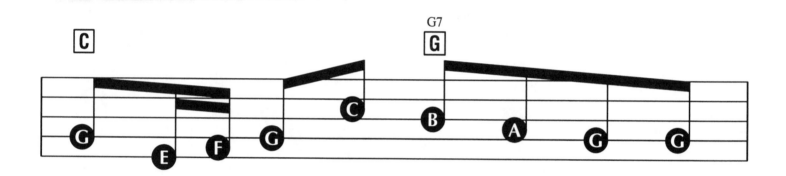

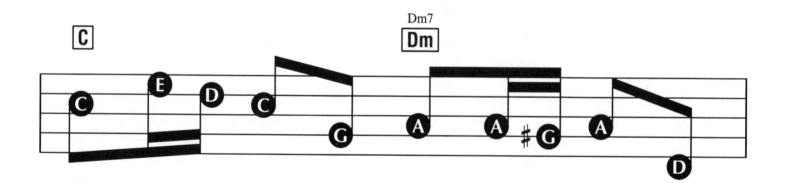

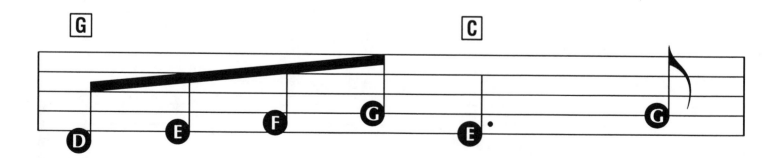

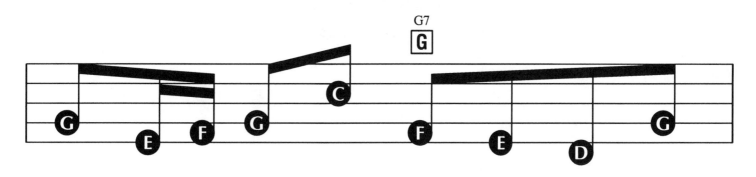

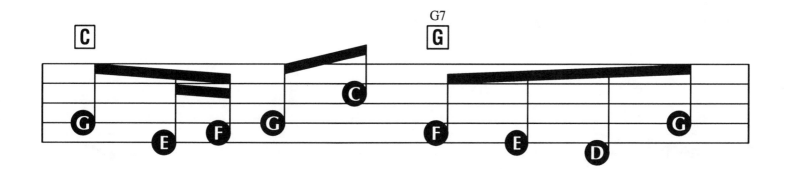

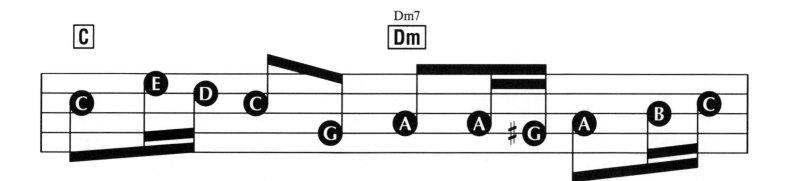

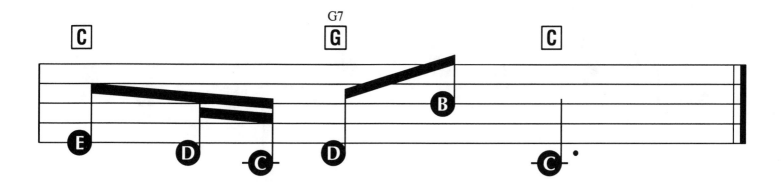

Nimrod
from ENIGMA VARIATIONS

Registration 2

By Edward Elgar

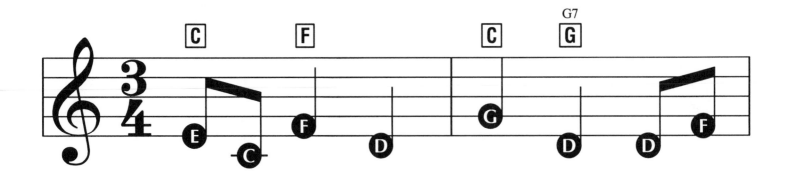

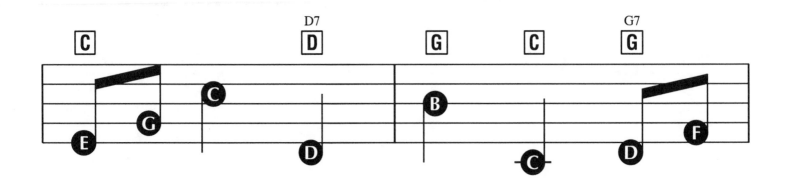

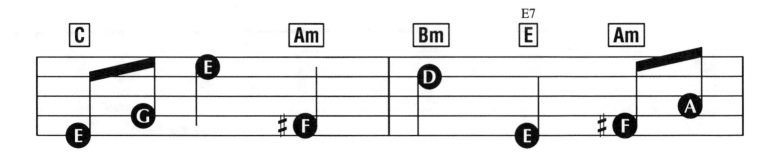

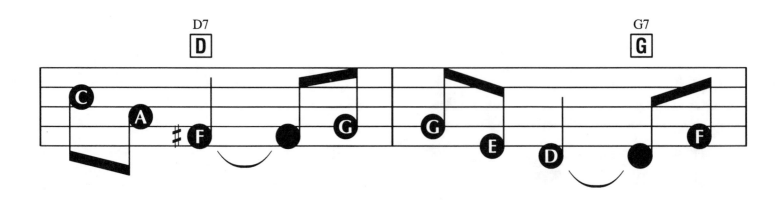

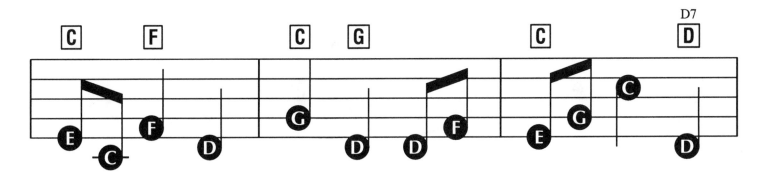

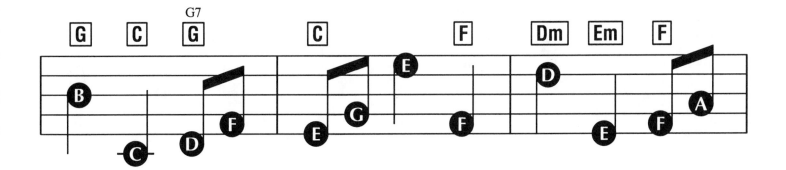

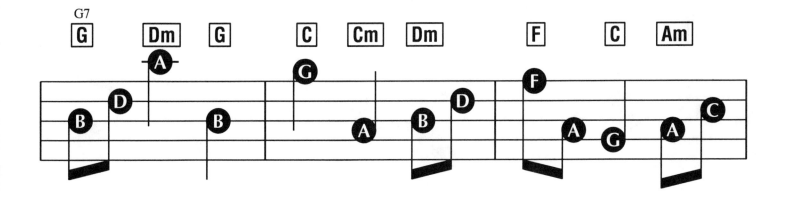

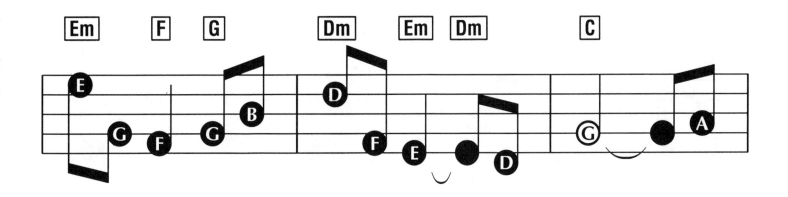

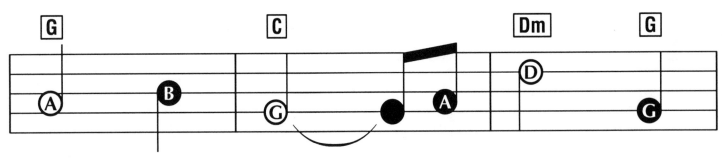

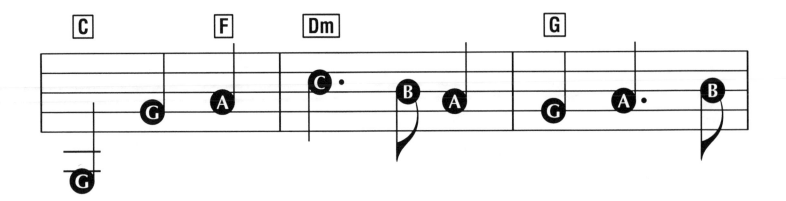

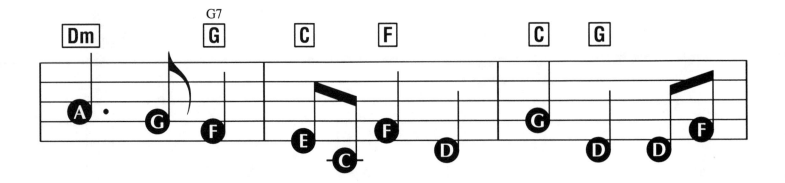

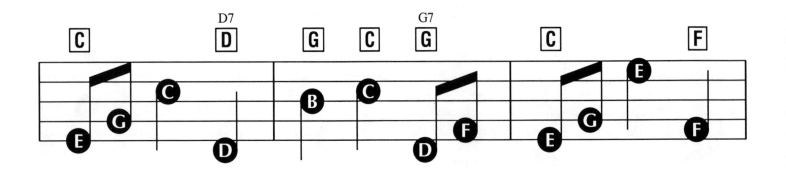

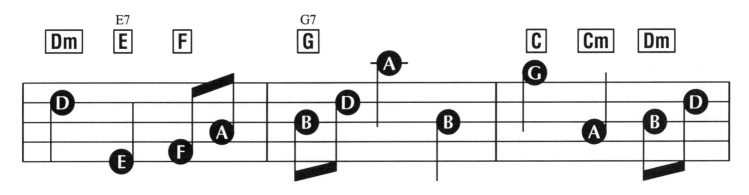

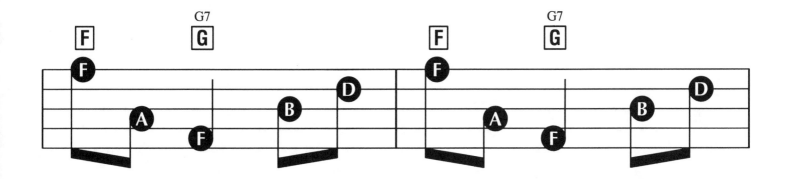

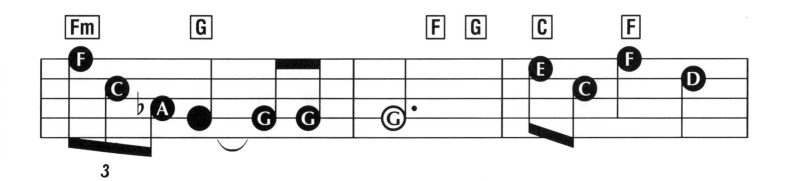

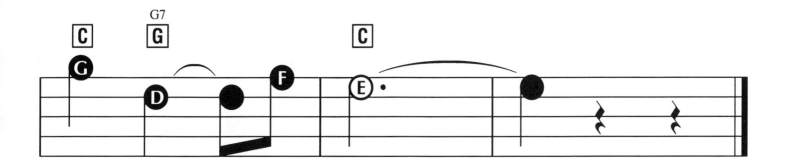

Panis angelicus
(O Lord Most Holy)

Registration 1

By César Franck

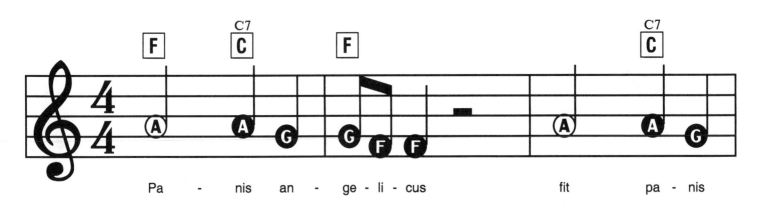

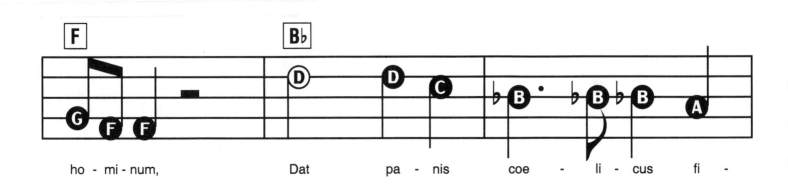

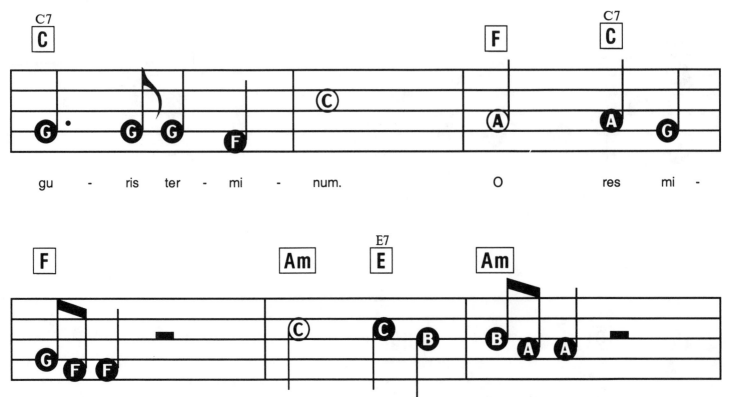

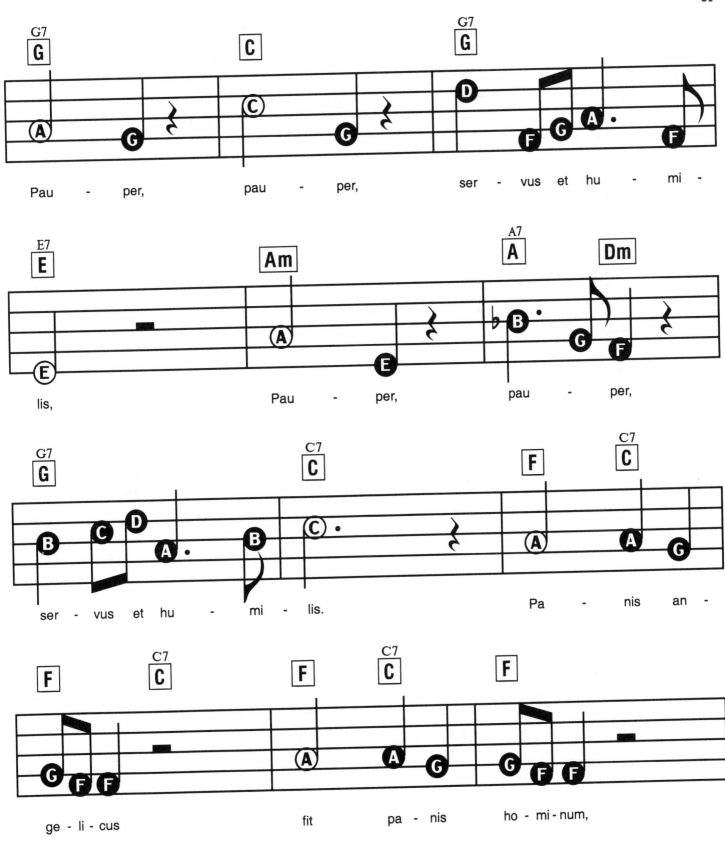

Pau - per, pau - per, ser - vus et hu - mi -

lis, Pau - per, pau - per,

ser - vus et hu - mi - lis. Pa - nis an -

ge - li - cus fit pa - nis ho - mi - num,

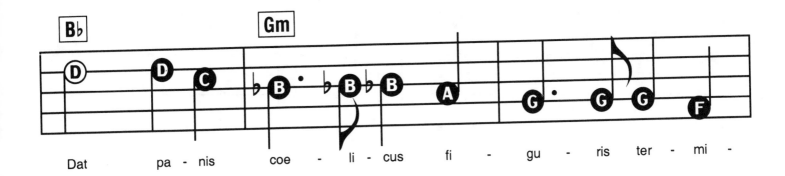

Dat pa - nis coe - li - cus fi - gu - ris ter - mi -

52

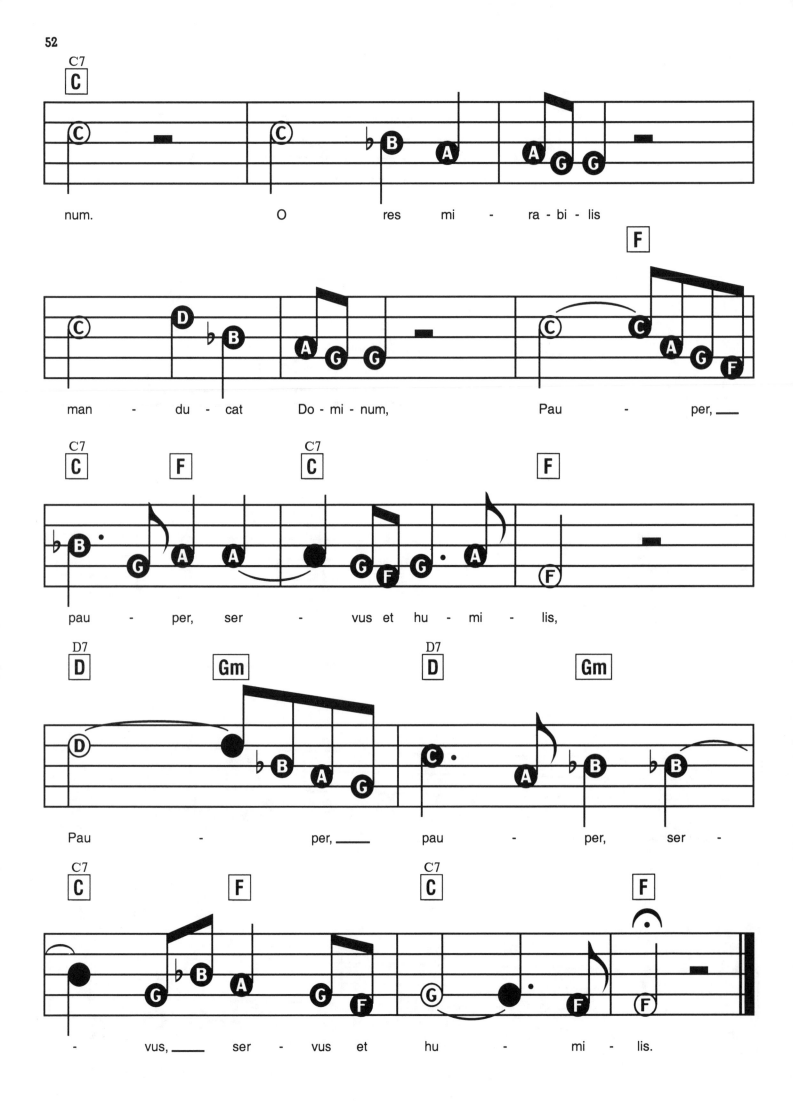

Rondeau

Registration 7
Rhythm: March

By Jean-Joseph Mouret

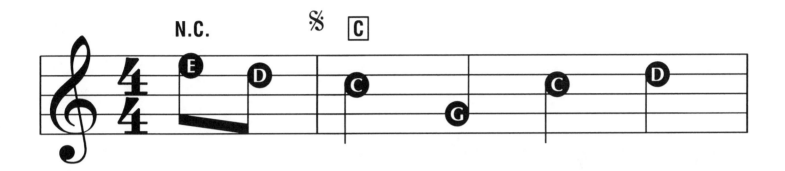

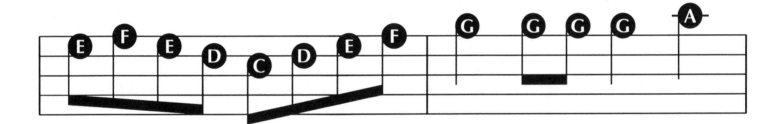

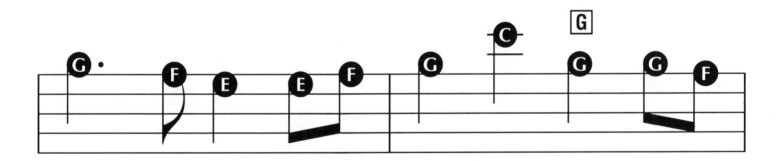

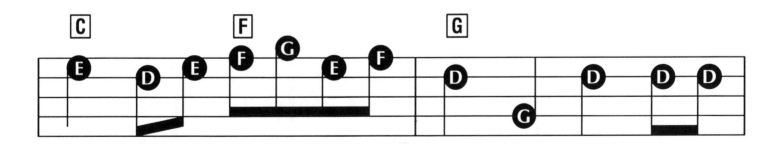

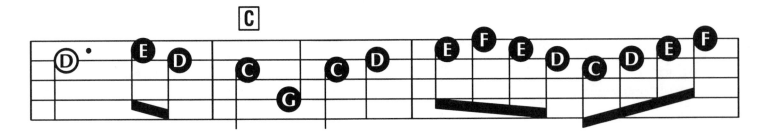

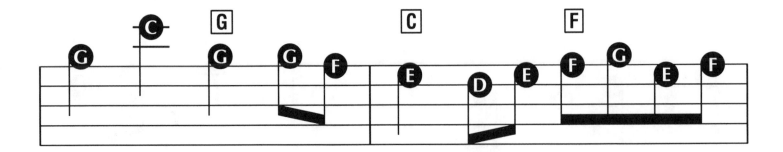

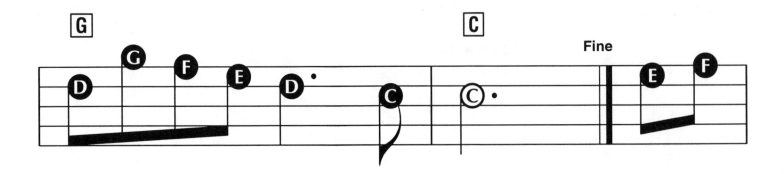

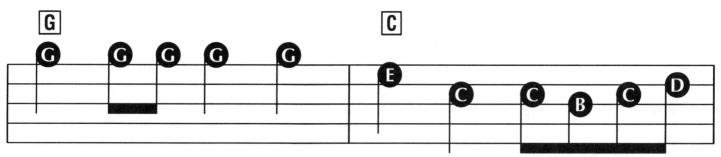

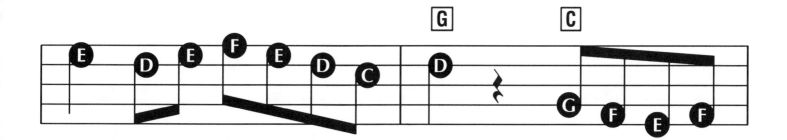

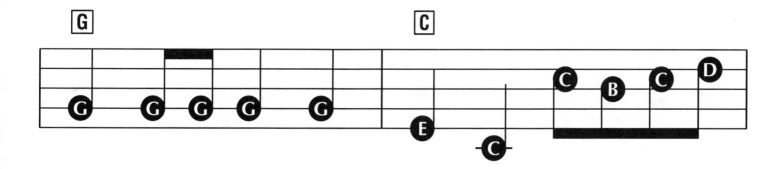

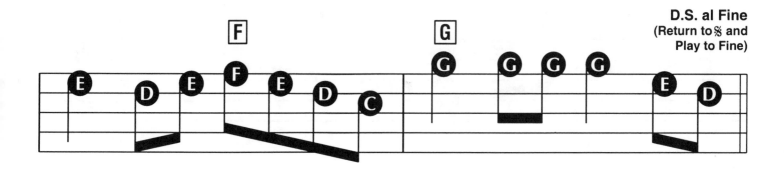

D.S. al Fine
(Return to 𝄋 and
Play to Fine)

Sheep May Safely Graze
from CANTATA 208

Registration 1

By Johann Sebastian Bach

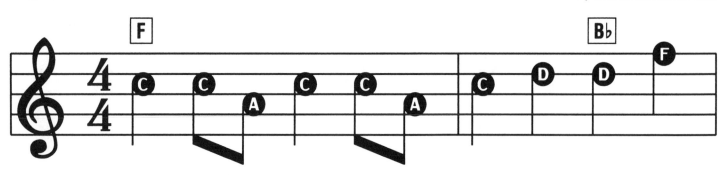

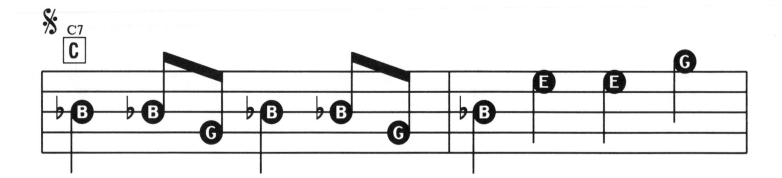

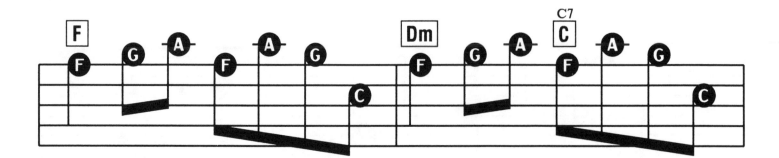

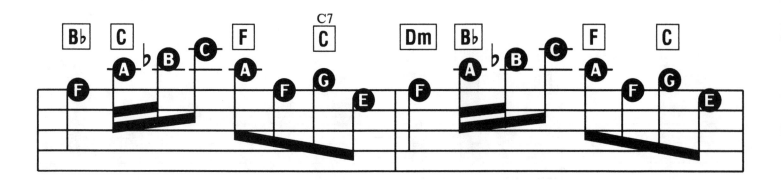

57

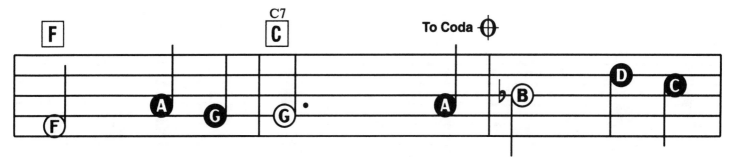

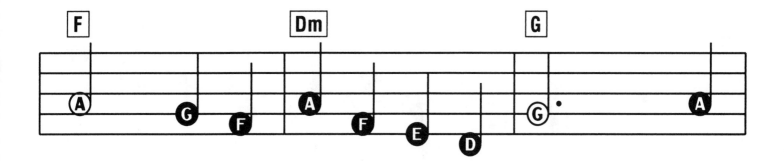

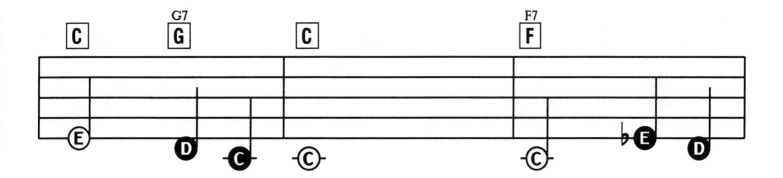

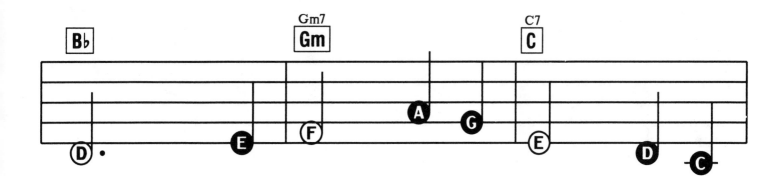

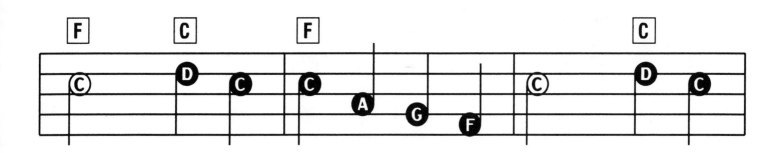

58

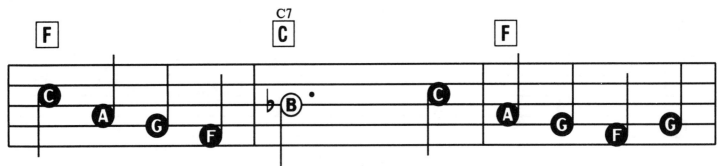

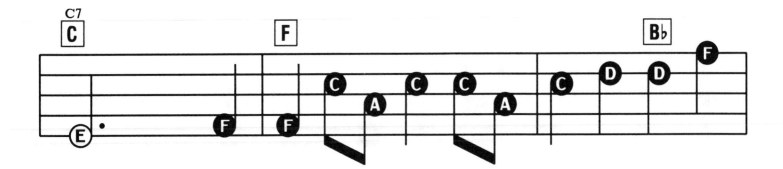

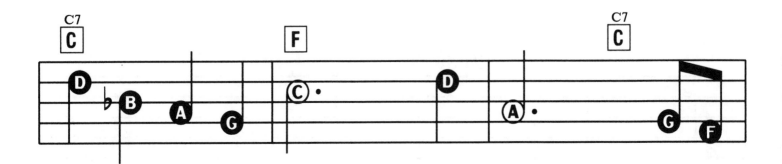

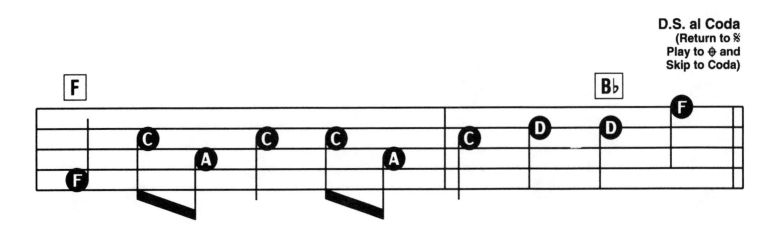

D.S. al Coda
(Return to %
Play to ⊕ and
Skip to Coda)

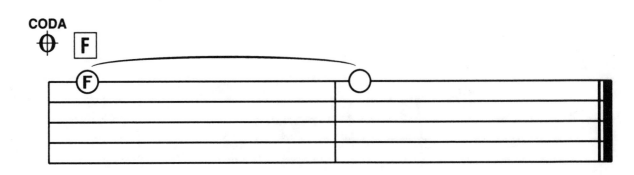

CODA

Trumpet Voluntary

Registration 7

By Jeremiah Clarke

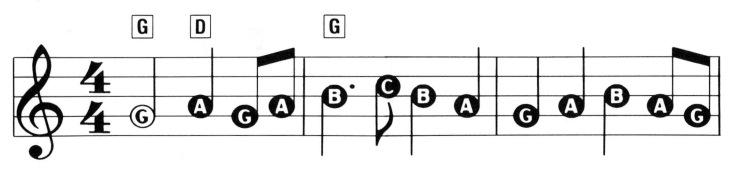

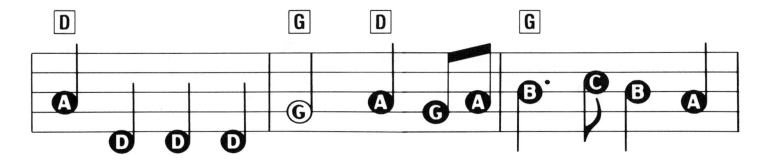

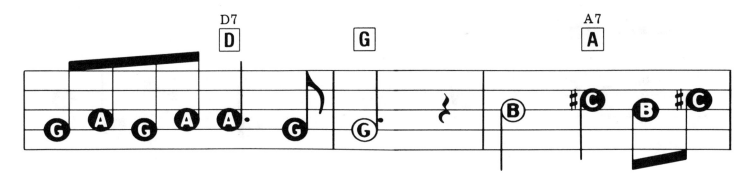

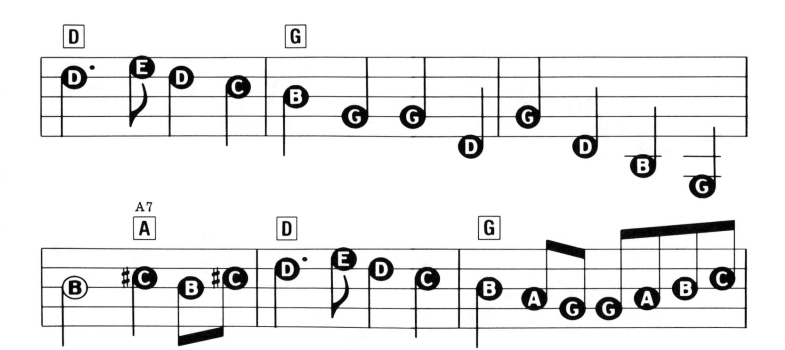

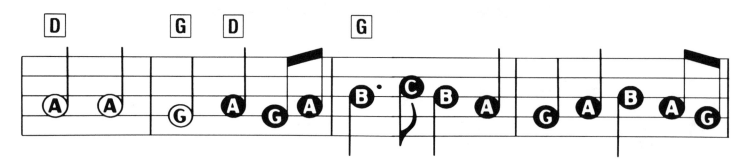

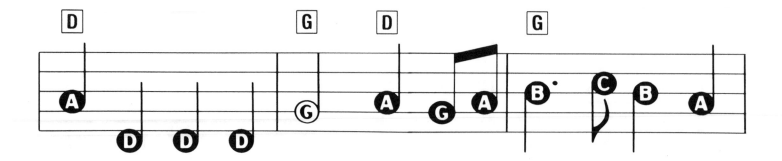

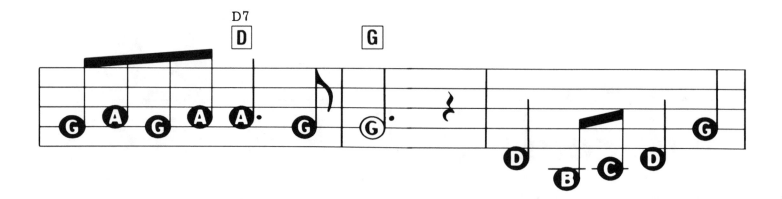

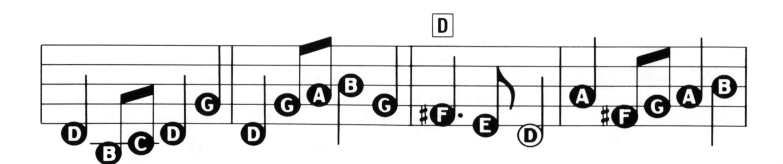

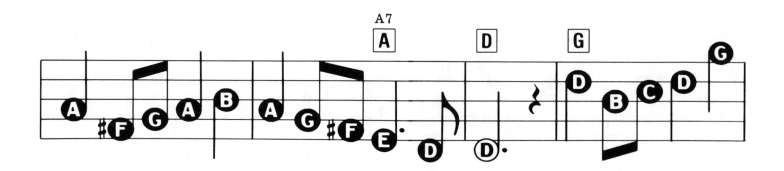

61

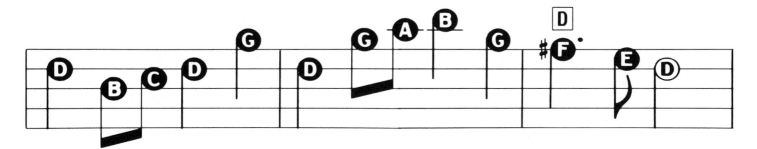

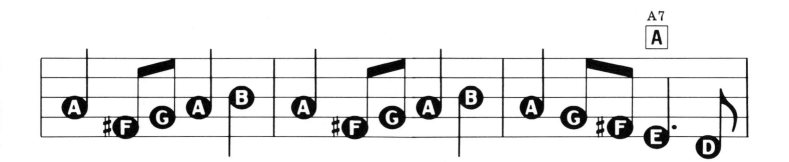

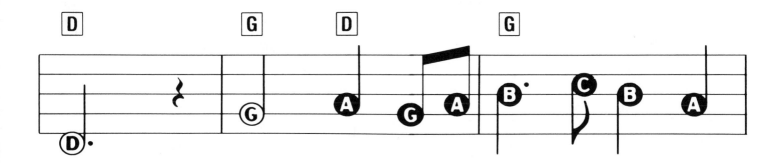

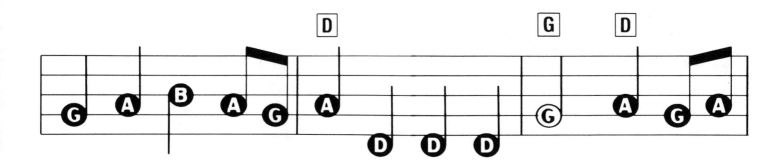

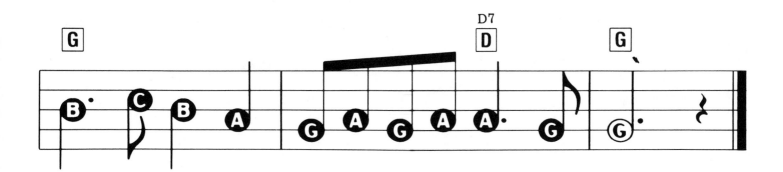

Trumpet Tune

Registration 7

By Henry Purcell

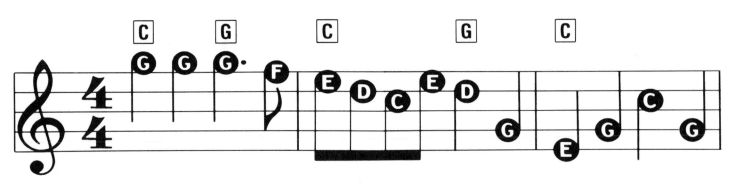

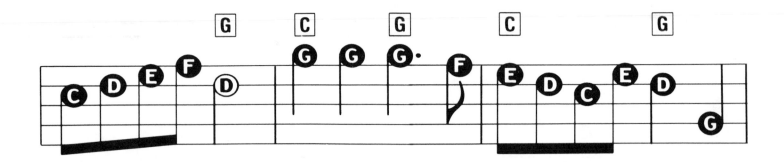

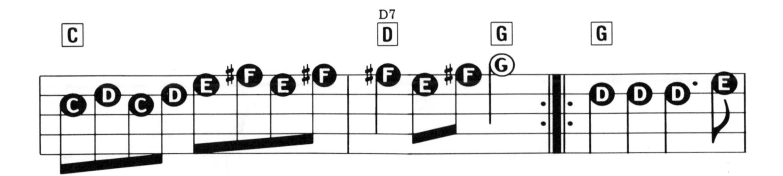

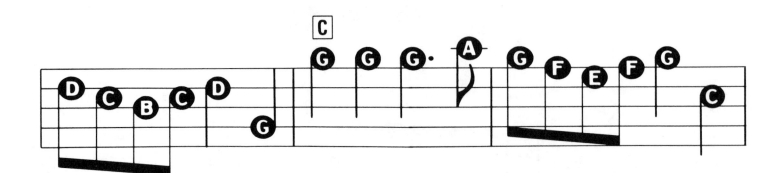

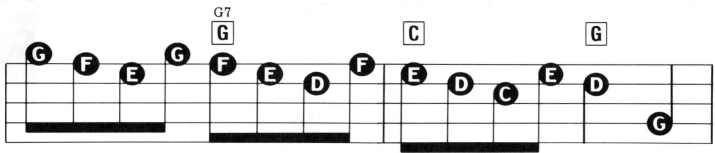

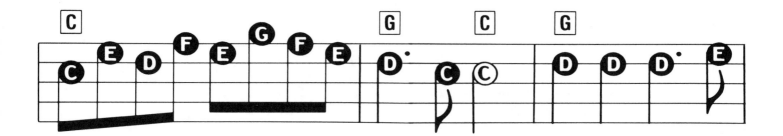

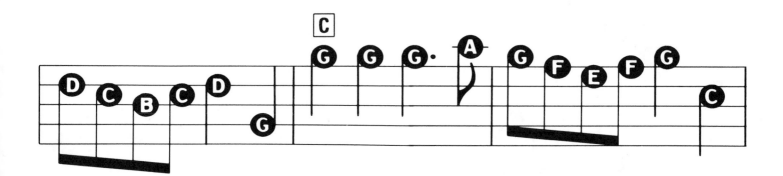

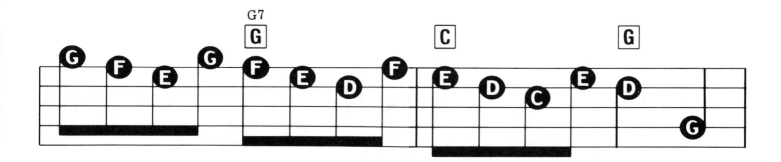

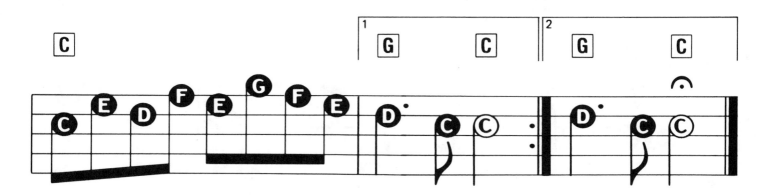

Wedding March
from A MIDSUMMER NIGHT'S DREAM

Registration 6

By Felix Mendelssohn

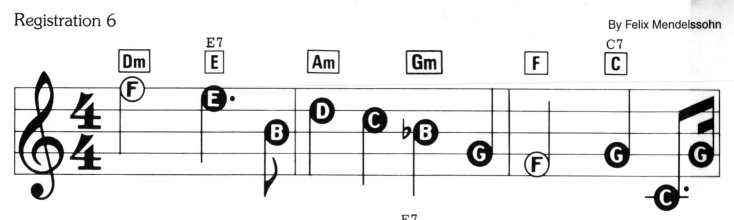

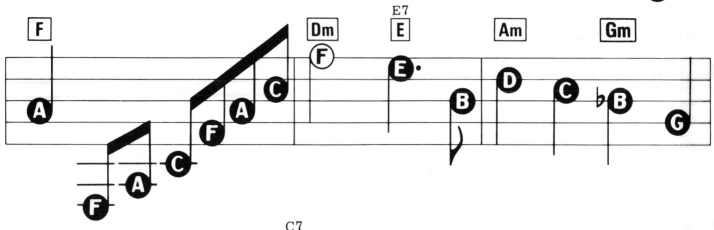

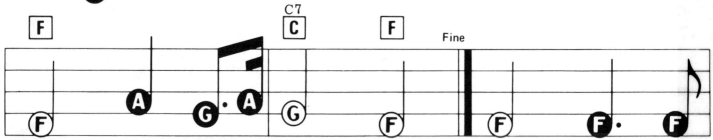

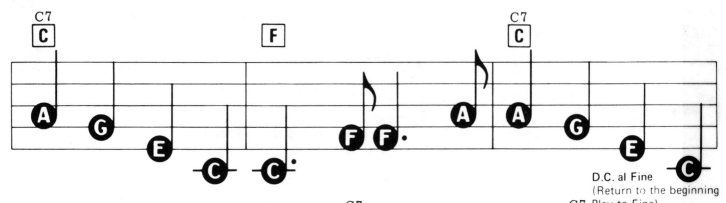

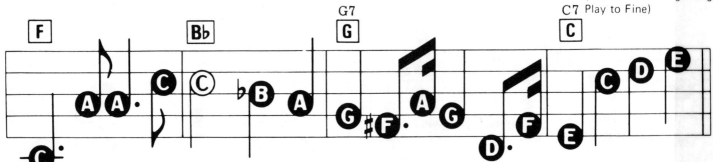